The Doge's Palace
in Venice

Michela Knezevich

The Doge's Palace in Venice

Electa

How to use this guide

Introduction
The first part of the guide gives a brief historical outline of the building and growth of the Doge's Palace.

The Visit
Starting from the second floor, the next part of the guide gives a description of the rooms in the order in which the visitor will see them.
This section is preceded by the plans of each floor. These are shown in the order in which they will be seen, thereby allowing easy identification of each room.

Appendix
The last part of the guide describes the Ducal Apartment and the Picture Gallery, which are not included in the previous section. Then there is a list of the doges of Venice and a selected bibliography.

On the cover
Gaspare Vanvitelli, *The Bacino of San Marco with the Molo, Piazzetta and the Doge's Palace*, detail. Madrid, Prado Museum.

Translation
David Stanton

© 1994 by **Electa**, Milan
Elemond Editori Associati

Contents

Historical Introduction

It was the recurrent barbarian migrations from the east which forced the inhabitants of the *X regio Venetia et Histria* (tenth region of Venetia and Istria) to seek refuge by fleeing from the largest and most flourishing towns such as Altino, Aquileia and Concordia to the Adriatic coast. This consisted of strips of muddy land which were flat and often submerged by water and covered a much greater area than that of present-day Venice; it may already have been partially inhabited by populations living a primitive existence who were, however, able to build shelters that were originally temporary, but later became permanent for those who, because of the repeated devastation, no longer hoped to return to their former homes. In fact, at first the settlements only lasted long enough to save these peoples and their possessions from the frequent forays. It was only with the fall of the Western Roman Empire in A.D. 476 and the raids of the Visigoths, Vandals and Swabians that a real exodus began with the permanent settlement of the lagoons, especially at Grado, Mazzorbo and Torcello. While it is difficult to say exactly how these refugees were organized socially and politically at first, it is certain that within a relatively short space of time they were able to acquire a degree of independence owing to the abundant supply of fish, the salt trade and their maritime skills. Slowly but surely these more numerous and longer-lasting new settlements became outposts defending the Byzantine empire against Lombard domination; they were governed by *magistri militum* (military leaders), who derived their authority from the exarch of Ravenna and to whom the tribunes elected by the people were subjected. It was only in the 7th century

Opposite
Porta della Carta.

Anonymous, View of Venice, 15th century.

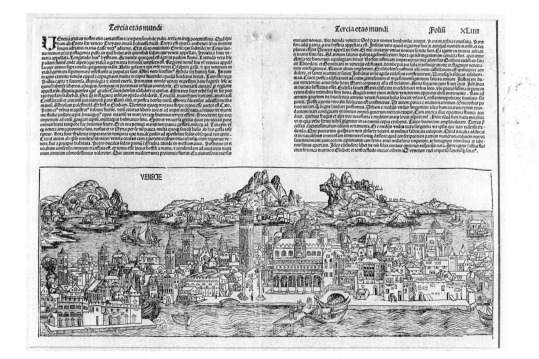

Renaissance façade.

that the institution of the *dux* (the much mythicized first doge), Paoluccio Anafesto, also with imperial consent, made the local government more independent, even if the claim by the chronicler Giovanni Diacono at the beginning of the 11th century that the existence of the doge was the result of a free election held by the Venetians cannot be substantiated.

The history of the 8th and 9th centuries was very complex due to the bitter power struggles between the families and factions. After an interval in which the tribunes gained the upper hand, in the mid-8th century, under Teodato Ipato, a return was made to the nomination of the doge, and this continued to be the case for an entire millennium of Venetian history. At this time the seat of government was moved from Eraclea to Malamocco. Finally, in the 9th century, even though it was not as outright as the Venetian historians claimed, there was the military victory over the Franks that thwarted their attempt to invade the lagoons under the command of Charlemagne's son Pepin, who wanted to replace the now much weaker Lombards. This success gave political substance to the Venetian settlement on the lagoons which, formally at least, continued to be under Byzantine authority, as was confirmed by the treaty of Aachen that brought the conflict between the Franks and the Byzantines to an end in 813. However, the remoteness of the capital favoured the independence of this far-flung province, the prestige of which grew as the Western Roman Empire fell into decline. In this period the autonomy of the city's government increased as it developed its trading activities and slowly but surely acquired a monopoly of commerce with the East thanks both to its special relationship with Byzantium and its astute policies. Neither was the religious aspect neglected: with the aim of reinforcing its independence, the city's Eastern patron saint,

Façade on the Molo.

Theodore was replaced by the apostle Saint Mark, who, historians later claimed, was predestined to have his mortal remains buried in Venice. The famous legend of the removal from Alexander in Egypt, thanks to the merchants Rustico da Torcello and Buono da Malamocco, of his body—covered with pork which the Muslims so detested—and its arrival in Venice, is narrated in the mosaics in the basilica of San Marco. His attribute, the winged lion, became the symbol of the Venetian Republic. In the 9th century the seat of government moved from Malamocco to the more sheltered area of Rivoalto, thereby marking the beginning of a new era for what was to become the "Most Serene Republic of Venice." In 810 Doge Agnello Partecipazio built the *palatium ducis* on a piece of land he owned on the islands of Rialto. The site was the one where the palace still stands, but the structure of the building is, obviously, no longer the same. The oldest known plan of the Saint Mark's area (13th century), redrawn by Tommaso Temanza in the 18th century, shows a building that was clearly defensive in nature: it was a quadrilateral with corner towers which included Partecipazio's house and the church of San Marco within a large perimeter. Today only faint traces of the corner towers are to be found: the first, a massive wall covered with marble slabs to the left of the Porta della Carta, links the palace to the basilica, while on the right an equally imposing structure set slightly further back suggests that this might have been a fortified entrance; level with this, the second tower marked the corner of the building facing the Bacino: this hypothesis is supported by the existence of stretches of wide foundations and the remains of a thick wall which appears to have been exposed to the elements, but is now incorporated in the interior of the palace. The third tower must have been situated at the corner facing the Ponte della Paglia, perhaps at a crucial point for the control of the river traffic which had been identified previously. In this case tradition comes to the aid of this hypothesis, since this part of the palace, both in contemporary accounts and in drawings, is always referred to as the *torresella* (little tower). No trace remains, however, of the fourth tower.

Scala dei Giganti, Mars.

In the 9th and 10th centuries Venice increased and consolidated its power, on the one hand with a shrewd mercantile policy which allowed it to obtain advantages for its sea traffic, bringing military aid to the Byzantine Empire which was in difficulty in its Southern Italian territories, on the other with its defeat of the pirates in the northern Adriatic, which assured it of supremacy on the seas. In the meanwhile the administration of the state, although it was still ruled by a doge, experienced a difficult period due to the repeated attempts of a number of families, sometimes successfully, to create a dynasty by attaching their sons to the government as co-regents. From 887 to 959 the Candiano family produced no less than four doges, but then Pietro Candiano IV was killed by rebels who set the palace on fire, causing its partial destruction. According to some accounts, it took about two years to rebuild it, while others maintained the reconstruction lasted at least fifteen years. Subsequently, under Doge Sebastiano

Scala dei Giganti, Neptune.

Courtyard of the Doge's Palace, 18th-century print.

Ziani (1172-78), the walls surrounding the castle were demolished; loggias and porticos appeared to be the architectural features which were more suited to an increasingly complex society where defence was no longer the overriding concern. The transformation of the institutions, with the creation of new officers of state who, by taking over some of the doge's functions limited his power, meant that a whole range of new chambers was needed to cater for the multiplicity of governmental and legal bodies. Thus, along the side facing the Piazzetta, the building *ad jus reddendum* (Law Courts) was constructed; this had a loggia on the first floor, while the offices were situated on the top floor. On the side facing the Molo was the *palatium commune*: the building where the assemblies of the eligible patricians were held, this was formed by using the external wall of the old castle as an internal wall; one end extended towards the Piazzetta while the other was located near the tower at the corner by the Ponte della Paglia. Little has survived of this building apart from remains of the footing of a wall in Istrian stone and a floor in terracotta tiles forming a herringbone pattern on two levels, while a column which can be dated with certainty to the 12th century has also been found incorporated in a wall that was built much later on, thus making the various hypotheses relating to the Palazzo dello Ziani appear to be even vaguer and more contradictory.

An important change in the political life of Venice which took place in 1297, usually referred to as the *Serrata del Maggior Consiglio* (the "closing" of the membership of the Great Council), resulted in an increase in the number of those having the right to participate in the legislative assembly. According to this innovatory formula there were two eligible categories, naturally belonging to the order of the patricians, the only one which had political power: those who had been members in the

Courtyard, view towards the Basilica of San Marco.

Loggia Foscari.

previous four years and those who had been chosen by three electors who also belonged to the Great Council and who had received at least twelve votes in the ballot of the Quarantia, which met with a quorum of thirty people. In this way the new law gave the members of the nobility who had been excluded from political activity due to financial difficulties the chance to return to it. From then onwards no other family was able to join the important assembly. But because the number of members of the Great Council rose from 400 to 1,200 a larger meeting hall was required. Both the possibility of maintaining the ground floor location of the hall, incorporating other rooms into it, and that of a new structure on the upper floor were taken into consideration. The three *sapientes* (sages) responsible opted for the latter solution, as may be seen in a document of late 1340. The work went ahead rapidly until 1348, when first the plague and then the war with Genoa hindered it. However, the building was completed in 1362: for the first time the names of those involved in the construction of the palace were mentioned in 1361—whether they designed it or were merely the builders is not known—when reference was made to the *tajapiera* (stonemason) Filippo Calendario and the *magister prothus* (chief architect) Pietro Basejo. The whole of the building facing the Molo was rebuilt, because the other rooms were also involved in the construction of the Sala del Maggior Consiglio and they were moved as a consequence. When the work had been completed the building looked very much as it does today. What remained of the Palazzo dello Ziani facing the Piazzetta, which was already very ancient at the beginning of the 15th century, was no longer suitable for the administration of justice. In 1424, under Doge Francesco Foscari (1423-57) it was decided to rebuild it, both because there was a danger that it might collapse and also so that it would

not look out of place next to the new building on the Molo. After the annual sum of 4,000 ducats had been allocated, it was decided that the new building should form the continuation of the rebuilt one, starting from the point at which the relief depicting Justice was situated (next to the thirteenth column of the loggia), so linking the end of the Sala del Maggior Consiglio to the main entrance of the palace, the one situated between the two imposing original buildings. The new building, with an arcaded ground floor, included loggias on the first floor open towards both the exterior and the courtyard; a huge chamber called the Sala della Libreria (later it was known as the Sala dello Scrutinio) completed it on the same floor as the Sala del Maggior Consiglio. Originally the internal loggia facing the courtyard was reached by the covered outside staircase known as the Scala Foscara, as may be seen in the engraving by Cesare Vecellio in *Degli habiti antichi et moderni di diverse parti del mondo* of 1590, and then another wooden staircase led to the Sala della Libreria. The large window with a balcony and the others repeat the motifs of the façade giving onto the Molo as well as the pinnacled crowning. The façade on the Piazzetta side was concluded with the construction of the Porta della Carta; built by Giovanni and Bartolomeo Bon, this was begun in 1438 and completed in 1442 — because this was later than the stipulated date the sculptors had to pay a penalty of a hundred ducats. Once this had been completed it proved necessary to rebuild the part of the palace into which it led; parallel to the building on the Molo, this was still the defensive structure of the early days. Thus, also the ancient buildings onto which it abutted were involved in the construction of the Foscari portico; this consists of six bays with ribbed cross-vaults, the keystones of which bear the carved figures of the Evangelists. It concludes on the east façade with a round arch with alternate bands of Istrian stone and red Veronese marble (on the extrados of the arch Foscari's coats of arms are a reminder that work was begun when he was doge). On the upper level there is a large niche with a four-centred arch, while the shelf which still surmounts the portal served as the plinth for a statue of the doge kneeling before the lion. That the work took a long time may be deduced from the presence of the insignia of Doge Cristoforo Moro (1462-71). A balcony with a parapet formed by balusters marks the division between the two floors. The construction is crowned by a spire with crockets projecting from the angles and pinnacles on which the statues of Saint Mark and the Arts stand. The work was completed under Doge Giovanni Mocenigo (1478-85). A devastating fire meant that it was necessary to rebuild the Doge's Apartment, which consisted of a series of rooms overlooking the Rio di Canonica; also the offices of a number of magistracies situated nearby were damaged. In September 1483 fire broke out in one of the rooms of the apartment and rapidly "the whole of the doge's palace was burnt down except one part" as Marin Sanudo reported in his *Vite dei Dogi*. Action was taken immediately: the doge's residence was moved to a house belonging to the Duodo on the other side of the canal which was rented for a hundred ducats per

Capitals on the exterior.

Opposite
Pinnacles on the Foscari Arch.

F. Hogenberg, *Fire in the Palace (after Lodewyck Toeput, called Pozzoserrato), detail, 1578.*

annum. There were numerous contrasting plans for the reconstruction: it was even proposed that the doge's residence should be built on the other side of the rio on a large area of land which would become available after the demolition of numerous buildings and would be linked to the Palazzo del Governo by a stone bridge, but nothing came of this, both because of the excessive costs involved and also because it was thought preferable for the doge to live inside the palace, above all for security reasons. The reconstruction on the same site of a building linking the Ponte di Canonica to the Ponte della Paglia seemed to be the best choice: work soon started under the direction of Antonio Rizzo, who designed and constructed the staircase which was built opposite the Foscari arch in accordance with the renewal project. The staircase was completed very rapidly, at least as far as the load-bearing structure was concerned, so that it was possible for Marco Barbarigo, who was elected as doge in 1485, to be crowned on the landing; this was the culmination of the ceremony in which the newly-elected doge was first presented to the people in the Basilica of San Marco, where he received the standard, then he was borne around the square in a type of litter called the *pozzetto* from which he threw coins to the onlookers; lastly he was invested with full power as doge by the placing on his head of the cap (*rensa*) by the youngest councillor and of the ducal crown (*zogia*) by the oldest one. Work on the façade giving onto the courtyard and canal was carried out at the same time as that inside the building and Marco Barbarigo's successor, his brother Agostino, was able to take possession of the renovated palace before his death in 1501: in fact, the first part of the reconstruction, which was carried out from the foundations upwards, had reached the second arch after the staircase in 1497, when Antonio Rizzo fled from Venice after he had been accused of embezzling a large sum of money from the funds allocated for the work. Although the Ducal Apartment was nearing completion, the same could not be said of the remaining part facing the Ponte della Paglia; while it was awaiting restoration maintenance was kept to a minimum, which was not sufficient to prevent it from falling into decay. After Rizzo's hasty departure "Master Pietro Lombardo, a man who is very skilled in his art" was put in charge of the works; under his direction the sculptural decoration of the façade and the Scala dei Giganti was executed. The fact that work on the palace made very slow progress was also due to the difficulties that the Venetian Republic faced in the early 16th century: the League of Cambrai, championed by Pope Julius II for territorial reasons regarding the Romagna and the Marches and composed of all the other Italian states, as well as a large number European ones (who regarded the League as an opportunity to destroy tthe Republic's political and economic power), resulted in a declaration of war against Venice which led to its crushing defeat at Agnadello in 1509. It appeared that the very existence of the Venetian state was in danger, but the victory near Padua the next year and the disagreement between the adversaries reversed the outcome of the war and saved Venice from ruin, although in the following years it felt the consequences, especially from an economic point of view. In 1515, when Antonio Abbondi, called Scarpagnino, succeeded Pietro Lombardo as chief architect of the palace, the situation was the same as in the previous years and also in the immediate future things did not change, so that work was limited to essential maintenance, while there was a serious risk that the administration of the state would grind to halt due to the bad state of repair of the building. The most important new feature to be added in this period was a covered wooden staircase "on the side of the new palace," which was the first step towards the building of the Scala d'Oro. It was only in 1531 that the decision was taken to reconstruct the old part of the palace, while another ten years passed before the corridor linking the doge's apartment to the Sala del Maggior Consiglio was built, so that the doge no longer had to make use of temporary wooden structures. In 1545 Francesco Donà became doge and it is his coat of arms on the marble façade, both on the ground floor and the upper floors that put the finishing touch to the work carried out in the eight years of his rule, while the work on the interior continued for a number of years.

Sculpture on a corner of the exterior, Archangel Michael.

Until 1556 the link between the buildings facing the canal (the one of the Barbarigo period and the Donà one) was formed by the wooden staircase mentioned previously, which was clearly unsuitable for the new structure. The project for the building of a new staircase was drawn up in 1544; after differing technical and political opinions had been listened to, the final choice from the five proposals presented was only made a year later; but in 1557 the work still proceeded slowly and was finished under the direction of the chief architect Pietro Piccolo in 1559, the year when Doge Lorenzo Priuli died and was succeeded by his brother Gerolamo. Numerous coats of arms of their family at different points on the staircase indicate the various stages of the work. After years of alterations, rebuilding work and extension, finally the palace could be considered complete: the legislative assemblies, the various government bodies, the doge's residence and the law courts were all now suitably accommodated, and the staterooms adequately reflected the might of the Venetian Republic. In effect it was the placing in 1565 of the two giant statues by Sansovino of *Mars* and *Neptune* at the head of the Scala dei Giganti which marked the conclusion of the building activity. The choice of these classical divinities was not a casual one; they were intended to symbolize in the eyes of those entering the palace the foundations of Venetian power, namely military action and domination of the high seas.

Sculpture on a corner of the exterior, Archangel Raphael.

This state of equilibrium did not last for more than ten years because in 1574, after a fire had smouldered for some time inside the building, the palace burst into flames, resulting in the destruction of some of the rooms on the second floor and the attics above: the rooms included the Sala delle Quattro Porte, the Anticollegio, the Collegio and the Senate. Fortunately the loading-bearing structures were not damaged and the funds immediately made available were used to restore the wooden parts and the attics and, above all, to completely replace the decoration in the damaged rooms: paintings, marble, wood

Scala dei Giganti, detail of the central arch.

Anonymous, Session of the revolutionary government on 2 April 1849. Lining the walls are the shelves of the Biblioteca Marciana, which was housed in the palace.

and precious ornaments. No sooner had the work on this part of the palace been completed than another fire broke out in the Sala dello Scrutinio, spreading to the Sala del Maggior Consiglio, where it completely destroyed the paintings by the Bellinis, Titian and Pordenone, as well as the roof. Because of the extent of the damage it was deemed expedient to consult about fifteen of the leading architects in the city: some of them, including Andrea Palladio, advocated the total rebuilding of the palace and the reconstruction of the façade, while others, such as Giovanni Antonio Rusconi, recommended that it should be restored as quickly as possible, with the original appearance being preserved. The Senate chose the latter solution. Meanwhile the meetings of the Great Council were held at the Arsenal. Unlike what had happened previously, the work proceeded rapidly and finished in 1579-80, under Doge Nicolò da Ponte. Apart from the doge's residence, the seat of government and the law courts, the Doge's Palace also housed the prisons on the ground floor, on both sides of the Porta del Frumento, where they remained until the second half of the 16th century, when Antonio da Ponte began the construction of the Prigioni Nuove (New Prisons), a building situated on the other side of the Ponte della Paglia; in 1600 it was linked to the palace by the Bridge of Sighs, built by Antonio Contin. After the prisons had been moved, a vast area was made available on the ground floor facing the Bacino: this needed to be renovated, but the reconstruction, under the direction of Bartolomeo Monopola, who had succeeded Contin, involved not only this area, but also the whole of the ground floor, where, after the demolition of the solid walls, an arcade similar to the one on the Renaissance façade was built. Also the Scala Foscara, linking the courtyard and the Sala dello Scrutinio, was demolished and replaced by the present in-

ternal staircase; in the empty space between the façade of the
Foscari arch facing the courtyard and the corner of the palace
Monopola built a two-tiered arcade surmounted by the structure containing a clock on the tympanum of which is engraved
the date 1615. This marked the conclusion of the architectural
history of the palace. The splendours of the past were rapidly
fading as a result of the difficulties in which the ruling class
found itself, so that at the beginning of the 18th century, with
its prestige on the decline, it made a last-ditch attempt to defend its privileges; nevertheless, as long as Venice remained
an independent republic, nothing could impede the function-
ing of the state. However, after Doge Ludovico Manin,
alarmed by rumours of conspiracy and revolt, convened the
Grand Council of the Republic on 12 May 1797 and abandoned
the insignia of office, the history of Venice changed radically,
likewise the uses and functions of the chambers in the Doge's
Palace. During the period of foreign rule—firstly Austrian,
then French, then Austrian once again—various government
offices occupied a large part of the palace: in 1807 the appeal
court was established there; in 1812 the Biblioteca Marciana
(Saint Mark's Library) was moved to the Sala del Maggior
Consiglio and the adjacent corridor and rooms, while the archaeological collections were placed on shelving along the wall
under the painting of *Heaven* and under the large windows on
the west side. In 1821 the Superintendency of Public Buildings
ordered the offices to leave the palace and, once the law courts
had been moved, the Sala dello Scrutinio was also occupied by
the library. For safety reasons, in 1827 this was moved to the
rooms of the Ducal Apartment; twenty years later this was
opened to the public as a museum. The stock exchange was located on the ground floor, as was the chamber of commerce,
while the Institute of Science, Letters and Arts occupied the
rooms of the armoury. Not even when Venice became part
of Italy in 1866 did the situation change. The continuous use of
the building, the weight of the bookshelves and the lack of
maintenance, due to which during heavy storms rain poured
into the rooms, had all helped to reduce the historic palace to a
precarious state. In the 1870s major restoration work was carried out, but it was only in 1899, because of the imminent danger of collapse, that the books were moved to the Sala del Pio-
vego on the floor of the loggias and in 1908 the library returned to its rightful home in the Libreria Sansoviniana; finally in
1919 the archaeological museum left the palace. In 1924 an
agreement was drawn up between the state, owner of the
building, and the municipality of Venice, according to which
the Doge's Palace would be managed by the municipality as a
museum open to the public. At present the offices of the Venice Superintendency of Ancient Monuments are located in the
part facing the Molo, while the museum offices are housed in
the side along the Rio di Canonica on the floor of the loggias.
In order to explain the significance of the names of the various
rooms in the Doge's Palace and the functions of the offices
which were situated there, I have thought it useful to refer
briefly to the complex organization of the Venetian government when describing the rooms themselves.

Antonio Rizzo, Eve

Antonio Rizzo, Adam

Ground floor

1. Porta della Carta
2. Porticato Foscari
3. Foscari Arch
4. Scala dei Giganti
5. Courtyard
6. Cortile dei Senatori
7. Scala dei Senatori
8. Riva Barbarigo
9. Riva Barbarigo
10. Pozzi
11. Riva Donà
12. Scala dei Censori
13. Porta del Frumento
14. Museum of the Opera del Palazzo
A. Albergeto's well
B. Nicolò dei Conti's well

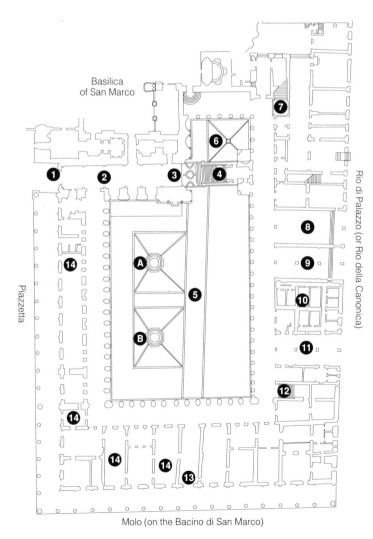

Plan of the ground floor

Second floor

15. Scala d'Oro
16. Atrio Quadrato
17. Sala delle Quattro Porte
18. Sala dell'Anticollegio
19. Sala del Collegio
20. Sala del Senato
21. Antichiesetta
22. Chiesetta
23. Sala del Consiglio dei Dieci
24. Sala della Bussola
25. Sala dei Tre Capi
26. Sala degli Inquisitori
27. Armoury
28. Passage leading to the
    Piombi and the Torture
    Chamber

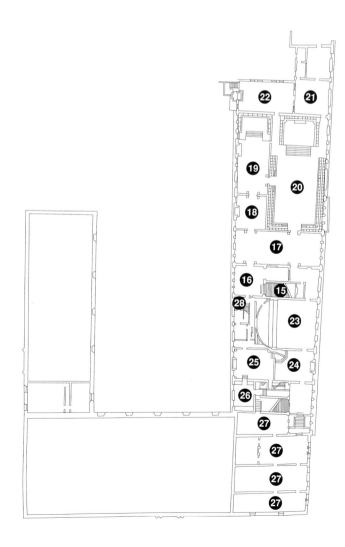

Plan of the second floor

First floor

29. Liagò
30. Sala della Quarantia Civil Vecchia
31. Sala dell'Armamento or Sala del Guariento
32. Sala del Maggior Consiglio
33. Sala della Quarantia Civil Nuova
34. Sala dello Scrutinio

Ducal Apartment

44. Sala degli Scarlatti
45. Sala dello Scudo
46. Sala Grimani
47. Sala Erizzo
48. Sala degli Stucchi or Sala Priuli
49. Sala dei Filosofi
50. Sala dei Leoni
51. Sala Corner
52. Sala dei Ritratti
53. Sala degli Scudieri
54. Sale Magistrato alle Leggi
55. Sala della Quarantia Criminal

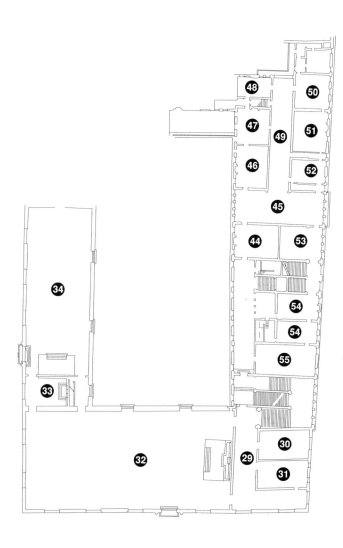

Plan of the first floor

Floor of the loggias

*Plan of the floor
of the loggias*

The Visit

A visit to the Doge's Palace can begin with the observation of the series of 14th-century sculptures on the façade giving onto the Molo, starting from the corner by the Ponte della Paglia: these consist of sculptural groups located at the corners of the palace and capitals on the columns of the arcade representing faces, both human and fantastic, vices and virtues, animals, historical personages and planets. The corner sculptures have been attributed to such Lombard artists as the Raverti and the Bregno and also to Filippo Calendario, who probably also designed the Gothic palace. Starting from the Ponte della Paglia, at the top is represented *Tobias and Raphael* (the travelling archangel), below the *Drunkenness of Noah* (allegory of indulgence). On the corner by the Piazzetta, at the top is *Michael* (the warrior archangel), below *Adam, Eve and the Serpent* (allegory of human frailty). Of the **capitals** it is interesting to note the one known as the *Sages* (looking at the façade on the Molo it is the second from the left) one of which bears a tablet with the date 1344, which refers to the period when this wing of the palace was built. In the centre of the façade on the Molo, restored after the fire of 1577, the large balcony with pilasters, niches and pinnacles was executed by Pietro and Paolo delle Masegne (1404) under Doge Michele Steno (1400-13). In 1579 the crown was remade and the statue of Venice as *Justice* by Alessandro Vittoria was added; in the 18th century Gian Battista Pellegrini remade the statue of *Saint George*. On the façade on the Piazzetta the first seven capitals date from the 14th century, as do the preceding ones since they belong to the same building, while the following ones, except for two, are 15th-century replicas of those on the Molo. On the quatrefoil of the loggia above the thirteenth column is sculpted a tondo representing *Justice* in the form of a female figure holding a sword in her left hand, sitting on two

Opposite
Scala dei Giganti

Sculptures on the corners of the exterior: (below left) *The Drunkenness of Noah and Adam;* (below right) *Eve and the Serpent.*

*Balcony on the façade
on the Piazzetta.*

*Scala dei Giganti, detail
of a side.*

lions grasping *Wrath* and *Pride* in their paws, while in the car-
touche held in Justice's left hand is the inscription: FORTIS/
IUSTA/TRONO/FURIAS/MARE/SUB PEDE/PONO. The **balcony** facing the Piazzetta, by an unknown sculptor, was executed before 1536 on the model of the one facing the Molo.
In the centre there was formerly a statue of Doge Andrea
Gritti (1523-38), but this was destroyed on the fall of the Venetian Republic in 1797 and replaced by a copy made by Giovanni
Botasso surrounded by mythological figures. As a result of
the fire in 1577 the sculptures on the top of the balcony fell
down and Alessandro Vittoria was commissioned to replace
them. The sculptural group at the corner of the Porta della
Carta represents, at the top, *Gabriel* (the archangel of peace),
below the *Judgement of Solomon* (allegory of wisdom). The
authorship of this latter work is a topic of scholarly dispute: it
has been variously attributed to Nanni di Bartolo, Jacopo della Quercia and Bartolomeo Bon; given the evident similarities
to other works by the latter, he is the most likely candidate.
The overall impression is that the sculptures form part of a
scheme involving motifs which are, in effect, a summary of
the fundamental norms of Venetian society: Commerce, War
and Peace can be related to the figures of the archangels,
while Indulgence, Impartiality of Judgement and Good Government are linked to the biblical events narrated on the corners of the palace. We now come to the **Porta della Carta**, the
main entrance of the palace; started in 1438 and completed
four years later, this portal was executed by Bartolomeo Bon,
whose signature is on the architrave. The name of the door
(literally "Door of the Paper") probably derives from the presence here of public scribes or the proximity of archives of
state documents (*cartarum*). Originally polychrome, it is a

synthesis of the Venetian Flamboyant style. The decorative scheme becomes increasingly clear as it is observed from the bottom upwards: the four virtues are placed in the niches of the plasters with, in the lower ones, *Temperance* and *Fortitude* and, in the upper ones, *Prudence* and *Charity*; these are all attributed to Antonio Bregno. In the overdoor is a sculptural group representing Doge Francesco Foscari (1423-57), under whom the construction of the door began, kneeling before the Lion of Saint Mark. This is a copy by Luigi Ferrari, dating from 1885, of the original by Bartolomeo Bon that was destroyed on the fall of the Republic in 1797; of this only the doge's head, now kept in the palace, has survived. Also by Bon are, in the central roundel, the bust of *Saint Mark* borne by three angels and, above this, the seated figure of *Justice* with the customary symbols of the sword and scales. The figure must have been much more prominent before the construction of the wall behind it; this belongs to the 18th-century Scala dello Scrutinio. Entry to the palace is through the **Foscari portico**, built in 1440-50; with its gloom it is in sharp contrast to the luminosity of the Scala dei Giganti in front of the Renaissance façade of the palace. In niches at the sides of the east façade of the **Foscari arch**, which is opposite the Scala dei Giganti, are placed bronze copies of the marble statues by Andrea Rizzo representing *Adam* and *Eve* (the originals have been removed). However, the sculptures of the Doges Cristoforo Moro (1462-71) and Giovanni Mocenigo (1478-85), which must have been located on the upper part of the arch, no longer exist. On the south façade, giving onto the courtyard, there is a copy of a soldier bearing a shield (the original of this, also by Rizzo, is now in the palace too); instead of the present apotropaic shield, not the original one, he must have borne one

Scala dei Giganti, detail of the balustrade.

Scala dei Giganti, side arch with Barbarigo coat of arms.

Scala d'Oro, details
of the stuccoes.

with the insignia of Doge Cristoforo Moro. On the same side, in another niche, there is a statue of *Francesco Maria I della Rovere* (1490-1538), donated to the Republic by his grandson Francesco Maria II, a general in the service of Venice, in 1625. The two **well curbs** in the courtyard of the palace date from the mid-16th century; each bears the signature of its respective founder: Nicolò de' Conti and Albergeto. While for the former there is no difficulty regarding the attribution, especially due to the analogy between this work featuring allegories involving water and another one, definitely his, for which there is printed documentation with the same motifs, the same cannot be said concerning the mysterious Albergeto, who is certainly not the founder of the culverin which is in the armoury. The **Scala dei Giganti** was designed by Antonio Rizzo and built in 1483-85; the decoration was completed around 1491. While it resembles the Gothic staircases of many Venetian palaces because it is both exterior and unroofed, the marble facing of the brick structure and the absence of a supporting wall mean that it is essentially Renaissance in style. Built on three arches, it is richly ornamented, with finely carved reliefs of *Fame* and *Victory* on the spandrels, while the risers of the steps are adorned with niello work. In particular,

Scala d'Oro

its monumental appearance can be ascribed to the statues of *Mars* and *Neptune* executed by Sansovino and standing at the head of the staircase in 1565. Nothing is known about the placing of the large *Lion of Saint Mark* on the façade of the palace above the Scala dei Giganti. The present lion is a copy executed by Luigi Borro as a replacement for the one destroyed in 1797.

On the left of the staircase is located the courtyard known as the **Cortile dei Senatori**; possibly this is where senators waited for government meetings. The south façade was designed by Giorgio Spavento in the early 16th century; the ground floor consists of arches echoing those conceived by Rizzo for the adjacent façade, while the first floor is embellished by a series of windows framed by columns and surmounted by tympanums with rich decoration in polychrome marble; here was located the chapel of San Nicolò, the doge's private oratory, formerly decorated with frescoes by Titian. The façade terminates with the marble balustrade of the balcony that is linked to the Doge's Apartment.

Scala d'Oro, detail of one of the frescoes.

The two flights of the **Scala dei Senatori** lead to the loggia; besides the lions' heads inserted in the wall, here may be noted the tablet made by Alessandro Vittoria commemorating the visit of Henry III, the king of France, to Venice; this was, so it seems, more the result of French insistence than the will of the Venetians. Further on is a tablet bearing the indulgence granted by Pope Urban V in 1362 to those who prayed in the church of San Nicola for the prisoners in the palace. The offices of various magistracies give onto the loggia of the Gothic wing facing the Molo (they are now used by the Soprintendenza ai Beni Ambientali e Architettonici di Venezia). The loggia facing the Piazzetta, also known as the **Loggia Foscara**, with Gothic capitals and buttresses, was used during the ceremonies for the solemn entry to the palace of various dogaresse as a gallery for displaying the products of the guilds. Approximately halfway along the loggia on the Renaissance façade is the **Scala d'Oro**. Designed in c. 1538 by Sansovino under Doge Andrea Gritti (1523-38), whose coat of arms may be seen over the arch, it was completed under the direction of Antonio Abbondi, called Scarpagnino, in 1559 when Lorenzo Priuli (1556-59) was doge; his coat of arms is on the internal side of the arch. At the sides of the portal leading to the staircase two columns are surmounted by statues by Tiziano Aspetti: *Hercules Slaying the Hydra* and *Atlas Bearing the World*. The Venetians identified the Hydra with the Turk, their arch-enemy. The name of the staircase derives from the rich decoration with white and gold stuccowork on the vault that surrounds, with a system of interconnected frames, frescoes by Giovan Battista Franco (partially restored at the end of the 18th century); these depict, on the first flight of stairs, the *Glorification of the Defence of Cyprus and Crete* and on the second *The Virtues Necessary for Good Government*. On the left of the second landing is the portal leading to the **Ducal Apartment** and on the right the one giving access to the judicial offices. Statues by Francesco Segala of *Abundance* and *Charity* stand in niches on the second flight of stairs.

Atrio Quadrato
(Square Entrance Hall)

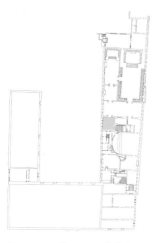

Francesco Bassano, Saint John Writing the Apocalypse. Atrio Quadrato.

This room, the entrance hall for the staterooms of the palace, was decorated under Doge Girolamo Priuli (1559-67), whose portrait executed by Jacopo Tintoretto in 1564-65 is placed on the ceiling. The artist has adhered to the official iconographic schemes of the palace: the doge, the personification of Venetian sovereignty, receives the sword from Justice in the presence of Peace under the watchful eyes of Saint Mark (or Saint Jerome?) and the ever-present lion. At the sides of this there are biblical scenes and Tintorettesque putti, allegories of the seasons that were originally associated with the artist's paintings formerly in the Atrio Quadrato and now in the Anticollegio. At present late 16th-century paintings

hang on the walls: *Saint John Writing the Apocalypse* and *Angel Announcing the Birth of Christ to the Shepherds*, attributed to Francesco Bassano, the *Expulsion of Adam and Eve from Paradise*, attributed to Paolo Fiammingo and the *Agony in the Garden* by an artist of the Venetian school.

Sala delle Quattro Porte
(Room of the Four Doors)

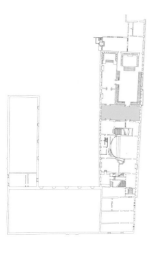

We now proceed to the Sala delle Quattro Porte, which occupies the whole width of the palace, so that on one side the windows give onto the Rio di Canonica and, on the other side, they overlook the courtyard. The College assembled here before the fire of 1574; after this it was the meeting place of the ushers.
The project for the restoration of this room that determined its present appearance was by Andrea Palladio and Giovanni Rusconi; it was realized by Antonio Da Ponte. The stucco decoration, by Bombarda, was executed in 1575-77. The frescoes on the ceiling were painted by Tintoretto in 1578-81 following a scheme conceived by Francesco Sansovino. The central panel depicts *Jupiter Entrusting*

Venice with the Domination of the Adriatic; in the tondi at the sides are *Juno Offering Venice the Peacock and Thunderbolt* and *Venice Surrounded by the Virtues Breaking the Yoke*.
In the eight ovals are depicted various cities and regions on the mainland: *Altino, Vicenza* (both repainted in the 18th century by Francesco Ruschi), *Treviso, Friuli, Padua, Brescia, Istria* and *Verona* (the latter was repainted in the 19th century by Antonio Paoletti). Andrea Palladio designed the four monumental doorways which give the room its name; each of them is surmounted by a marble group relating to the room to which it gives access. Thus, above the door leading into the Atrio Quadrato is *Secrecy Wrapped in a Cloak, Fidelity with a*

Double Flute and *Diligence with Pen and Papyrus* by Giulio Del Moro; over the door leading into the Anticollegio is *Vigilance with a Cock* between *Eloquence with the Moon, Snake and Caduceus* and *Facility of Speech with a Sparrowhawk and Wings* by Alessandro Vittoria; over the door leading into the Senate is *Minerva between Armed Warfare and Peace with an Olive Branch and Cornucopia* by Gerolamo Campagna; over the door giving onto the Consiglio dei Dieci is *Authority with Cupid Bearing the Sceptre between Religion Crowned with Stars and Justice with a Fasces and Camel* by Francesco Castelli.
On the wall adjacent to the Atrio Quadrato, on the right, is *Faith Adored by Doge*

Grimani. The painting, begun by Titian c. 1550 and still unfinished when the artist died, was completed by his nephew Marco Vecellio with the addition at the sides of the figures of a prophet and a standard bearer. On the same wall is the *Venetians under the Command of Gattamelata Defeating the Visconti and Reconquering Verona*, by Giovanni Contarini. On the opposite wall, on the left, hangs the *Legates of Nuremberg Receiving a Copy of the Venetian Laws from the Doge Leonardo Loredan in 1508*, painted by Carlo and Gabriele Caliari. In the centre is *The Doge and the Patriarch Welcoming Henry III, King of France, to Venice*, by Andrea Micheli, called Vicentino. The painting commemorates the Henry

Sala delle Quattro Porte.

Giambattista Tiepolo, Neptune Offering Venice the Riches of the Sea, detail. Sala delle Quattro Porte.

Andrea Vicentino, The Doge and the Patriarch Welcoming Henry III, King of France, to Venice, detail. Sala delle Quattro Porte.

III's visit to Venice when he arrived from Poland in 1574 and depicts the scene of his arrival at the Lido where Doge Alvise Mocenigo I and the patriarch Giovanni Trevisan are waiting to welcome him. The triumphal arch which is visible on the right was designed by Palladio; made of papier-mâché this was part of the special scenery constructed in the 16th century in Venice and other Italian cities for particularly important occasions.

Naturally the purpose of this painting is essentially a political one; since the Sala delle Quattro Porte was the anteroom for those waiting to be received by the doge, it allowed the ambassadors to reflect on the sagacity and diplomatic prowess of the Venetian rulers.

On the right is the *Reception in the Collegio of a Persian Ambassador in the Presence of Doge Pasquale Cicogna*, by Carlo and Gabriele Caliari. Above the windows facing the courtyard is *Venice Leaning on the World* by Niccolò Bambini (18th century).

A painting by Giambattista Tiepolo, *Neptune Offering Venice the Riches of the Sea*, executed c. 1740, which was a replacement for a ruined fresco by Jacopo Tintoretto, used to hang over the windows giving onto the Rio Canonica. At present it is displayed on an easel to allow it to be seen more easily; in place of the original there is a photographic copy.

Sala dell'Anticollegio (Antechamber of the College)

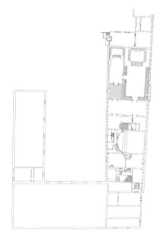

In our progress towards the presence of the Signoria we now come to the Sala dell'Anticollegio. Because this modestly sized room was involved in the fire of 1574 its decoration resembles that of the Sala delle Quattro Porte, with stuccowork and frescoes on the ceiling. The central fresco, *Venice Conferring Rewards and Honours*, was painted by Paolo Veronese. Besides the stucco decoration, Marco Del Moro executed the grisaille ovals representing *Abundance, Navigation, Justice* and *Meditation*. Two windows flank the imposing Palladian fireplace; at the sides of this Vincenzo Scamozzi added the two *Telamones*, while Tiziano Aspetti executed the relief in its centre representing *Venus*

Asking Vulcan for Arms. The walls, which were originally covered with gilded leather, were adorned with paintings in 1713, thanks to the bequest of Bertucci Contarini, who in 1595 willed that a number of his paintings should go to the Republic if the male line of his family were to become extinct. Thus, the *Rape of Europe*, executed by Paolo Veronese c. 1580, and the *Return of Jacob with his Family*, which Jacopo Da Ponte di Bassano painted c. 1574, became state property. The paintings, together with many others in the Doge's Palace, were taken to France after the fall of the Republic in 1797; they returned to Venice during the second period of Austrian domination in 1816. On the

Sala dell'Anticollegio, view towards the Sala del Collegio.

Jacopo Tintoretto, Mercury and the Three Graces. Sala dell'Anticollegio.

Jacopo Bassano, Return of Jacob with his Family. Sala dell'Anticollegio.

two walls on each side of the doors were hung the paintings which Jacopo Tintoretto executed in 1577-78 for the Atrio Quadrato: *Mercury and the Three Graces, Minerva and Mars, Bacchus and Ariadne* and *Vulcan's Forge*. The paintings represent mythological themes, each of them with a symbolic meaning: the Three Graces and Mercury represent Spring with the element Air (the clemency and wisdom of the state); Minerva who drives Mars away and protects Peace and Abundance represents Summer with the element Earth (wisdom keeps wars away from the state); Ariadne crowned by Venus and Bacchus represents Autumn with the element Water (the close relationship with the sea and the

sovereignty of Venice by divine will); Vulcan's forge with the Cyclopes represents Winter with the element Fire (the unity of the administration of the state and the armed forces). According to the Venetian historiographers the paintings are an allegory of the wise government of the Republic; modern scholars extend this reading to a cosmogony which identifies the harmonious succession of the seasons with the harmony of good government. This interpretation is all the more convincing if it is borne in mind that these canvases were originally hung in the Atrio Quadrato on the ceiling of which four monochrome putti symbolize the seasons.

Sala del Collegio
(College Hall)

Through the doorway surmounted by a marble group by Alessandro Vittoria representing *Venice between Concord and Glory* the visitor now comes to the Sala del Collegio. In Venetian political language *Collegium* was a generic term for many political or administrative councils. The same word referred to the Signoria (the chief political council formed by the doge, six councillors and the three heads of the *Quarantia. Manus* referred to smaller commissions elected by the Great Council and the Senate. They were usually composed of the Sages of the Council of the *Pregadi* (senators), the Sages of the *Terraferma* (mainland) and the Sages of the Orders. When the *Collegium* was combined with the three *Manus* the plenary College was formed. Among the numerous functions of this magistracy, which met every day except Sunday and Monday, that of preparing bills for presentation to the Senate was the most important because it gave it the power to influence the decisions of the latter organ. Moreover, with regard to certain topics, the College's decision overrode the vote of the Senate. Here foreign ambassadors were received, while the Venetian ones reported back here when they returned from their diplomatic missions.

The wood panelling on the walls, the tribune at the end and the carved ceiling were designed by Andrea Palladio and executed by Francesco Bello and Andrea Faentin, while in 1575-77 Veronese completed the paintings on the ceiling. This cycle follows a scheme that exalts the

Sala del Collegio, view towards the throne.

power and greatness of Venice: the rectangular panel near the door leading from the Anticollegio depicts the *Lion between Mars and Neptune*, the central oval *Faith, the Foundation of the Republic* and the panel near the tribune *Justice and Peace Offering the Sword, Scales and Olive Branch to Venice Enthroned*. The inscriptions that accompany the three larger canvases are clear evidence of the celebratory nature of the scheme. In the side panels are depicted the Virtues: *Fidelity with a Dog, Prosperity with a Cornucopia and a Caduceus, Meekness Stroking a Lamb, Vigilance with a Crane, Simplicity with a Dove, Dialectics with a Spider's Web between her Fingers, Reward* and *Moderation Plucking a Feather from an Eagle*. Between these paintings and the central ones there is a series of monochrome panels. Only the central canvases

have been attributed with certainty to Veronese. The painting over the tribune, *Sebastiano Venier Thanking the Saviour for the Victory at Lepanto*, also by Veronese, commemorates the famous naval battle in 1571. Composed as a loggia overlooking the battle scene, it represents Venier, commander of the Venetian fleet and future doge, kneeling in veneration of Christ and Saint Justina, while in the sketch in the British Museum the figure of Venier is given more prominence as he is about to be crowned doge by Venice (later depicted as Saint Justina) with the benediction of Saint Mark (then depicted as Christ). Besides, in the final version the doge's horned cap is held by Venice, who is, however, in the background. In this painting the focus is on the celebration of the victory rather than on the personal contribution of

(below left) *Paolo Veronese, Mars and Neptune. Sala del Collegio, ceiling.*

(below right) *Paolo Veronese, Justice and Peace Offering the Sword, Scales and Olive Branch to Venice Enthroned. Sala del Collegio, ceiling.*

Paolo Veronese, Faith, the Foundation of the Republic. Sala del Collegio, ceiling.

the commander. At the sides of the painting there are two monochromes representing *Saint Sebastian* and *Saint Justina* (the latter is often depicted in this context because the victory at Lepanto was won on her feast day, 7 October 1571), which can certainly be attributed to Veronese.

On the wall on the courtyard side of the hall, between the windows and various monochromes by artists in the circle of Veronese, is the monumental fireplace designed by Gerolamo Campagna, who also executed the statues at its sides of *Hercules* and *Mercury*. The paintings on the walls, executed in 1581-84,

are by Jacopo Tintoretto and his workshop. On the wall opposite the window, on the right, is the *Mystic Marriage of Saint Catherine Watched by Doge Francesco Donà Surrounded by Prudence, Temperance, Eloquence and Charity*, perhaps the only of these paintings for which Jacopo was directly responsible, at least as far as the composition of the scene and the saint's face are concerned, while the group of the Virgin and Child is probably the work of his son Domenico. In the centre is *Doge Nicolò Da Ponte with Saints Mark and Nicholas Invoking the Virgin who Appears between Saints Anthony Abbot and Joseph.*

On the left is *Doge Alvise Mocenigo I with Saint Mark and Other Saints Adoring the Redeemer and Evoking the Vow Made for the Cessation of the Plague of 1576*. On the wall opposite the tribune hangs *Doge Andrea Gritti with Saint Mark Adoring the Virgin Enthroned between Saint Bernardino, Saint Alvise and Saint Marina*. The subject is the same as that of the painting by Titian which was hung in the Senate in 1531 and lost in the fire of 1574, but naturally the composition of this version is different and the handling is typically Tintorettesque, based above all on the use of light effects. A clock set in the wall opposite the windows must certainly have existed in 1534, as a document relating to its maintenance informs us. It was damaged by the fire of 1574, but in 1576 mention was made of the need to find a reliable person to see to its upkeep, so it must have been in working order. The clock consists of a crown in pink Botticino marble moulded as a full torus; it is gilded externally and internally and subdivided into twenty-four sectors containing trapezoidal pieces of black marble bearing Roman numbers from I to XXIV in an anticlockwise direction and not shown in a subtractive position, which were both characteristics of early clocks. The central part of the face is in wood painted to imitate marble; the gilding is 17th century. At the sides of the clock and the two

Tintorettesque monochromes, representing the seasons and hence the passing of time, are carved and gilded wooden frames decorated with fruit and flower motifs. After 1574 all the wood panelling now present was reconstructed, while the bench on the tribune, the dais and the parapet date from the last century. After the fall of the Republic the secret meetings of the municipalists took place here, as F. Zanotto informs us. Subsequently the hearings of the court of appeal were held here, while from 1858 onwards Maximilian, Archduke of Austria, used it as his audience chamber.

Jacopo Tintoretto, The Mystic Marriage of Saint Catherine Watched by Doge Francesco Donà Surrounded by Prudence, Temperance, Eloquence and Charity, detail. Sala del Collegio.

Sala del Senato (Senate Hall)

Sala del Senato.

Like the preceding rooms, the Sala del Senato was restored after the fire of 1574. The government organ which met in it was one of the oldest Venetian institutions (it was created in the 13th century) and initially, under mandate from the Great Council, it was responsible for maritime affairs and trade, but the *Serrata* of 1297 led to the expansion of the Council and its transformation into a general assembly of the aristocracy, making it less effective in its functions. As a result the patriciate, which rejected the formation of a new body because of its innate conservatism, entrusted the Senate with its political powers. The number of its members grew after it had absorbed the Quarantia and the Council of Ten, the guardian of the constitution which was also responsible for state security, and as a result of the establishment of the *zonta*. A special committee set up by the Senate for the transaction of important business, the latter consisted of twenty nobles, with no more than one coming from the same family and not more than one per office. No sooner had the reasons for its formation ceased to exist than it was suspended, subject to annual confirmation. From 1506 onwards it was renewed automatically; meanwhile the number of extra members had grown to sixty. In the mid-16th century the Senate comprised about three hundred members because other magistrates, apart from those already mentioned, could join it. Not all those forming part of it had the

Jacopo and Domenico Tintoretto,
The Triumphal Exaltation
of Venice. Sala del Senato.

same rights: in fact, some had the power to initiate the legislative process and to vote, others only had one of these powers, others neither of them. The name *Pregadi* that was given to this institution derived from the fact that the doge "requested" (It. *pregava*) the members to participate in the sessions.

After the carved and gilded ceiling, designed by Cristoforo Sorte, had been finished in 1581, a start was made on the cycle of paintings on the ceiling and walls; this was completed in 1595 under Doge Pasquale Cicogna (1585-95). In the central panel on the ceiling there is the *Triumphal Exaltation of Venice*, conceived by Jacopo Tintoretto, but largely executed by his son Domenico. Towards the Sala delle Quattro Porte is *Doge Pasquale Cicogna Adoring the Eucharist*, by Tommaso Dolabella, while near the tribune is the *Masters of the Mint Striking Coins*, by Marco Vecellio. In the panels at the sides of the central one is, towards the College, *Venus Supervising the Work of the Cyclopes in Vulcan's Forge*, by Andrea Micheli, il Vicentino, and, towards the Rio, the *Doge Receiving Historians and Poets*, by Antonio Vassilacchi, called Aliense. In the corners, towards the Sala delle Quattro Porte, there is *Military Valour* and *Liberty* and, towards the tribune, *Eloquence* and *Truth*.

On the wall above the tribune, where the doge's throne stands, between two monochromes representing *Equity* and *Intelligence*, by Palma Giovane, hangs the enormous *Dead Christ Supported by Angels and*

Adored by Doges Pietro Lando and Marcantonio Trevisan with their Patron Saints, by Jacopo Tintoretto, although the artist's contribution was probably limited to the overall composition and the figure of Christ. Under this work, at the sides of the doge's throne, are the green monochromes *Demosthenes Haranguing the People* and *Cicero Accusing Catiline in the Senate*, executed by Domenico Tiepolo in 1775. On the wall opposite the windows there are the following paintings by Palma Giovane: *Obedience* (monochrome), *Venice Receiving Gifts from the Subject Cities Presented by Doge Francesco Venier* and the *Celebration of Doge Pasquale Cicogna*, in which the doge with Saint Mark beseeches Christ in the presence of Faith, Justice and Peace; in the background is

Above
Jacopo Tintoretto, Dead Christ Supported by Angels and Adored by Doges Pietro Lando and Marcantonio Trevisan with Their Patron Saints. Sala del Senato.

Below
Tommaso Dolabella, Doge Pasquale Cicogna Adoring the Eucharist. Sala del Senato, ceiling.

Opposite
*Jacopo Palma il Giovane,
Allegory of the Victory over
the League of Cambrai, detail.
Sala del Senato.*

(below left) *Jacopo Palma
il Giovane, Venice Receiving
Gifts from the Subject Cities
Presented by Doge Francesco
Venier, detail. Sala del Senato.*

(below right) *Jacopo Tintoretto
and assistants, Doge Pietro
Loredan Beseeching the Virgin
for the End of the Famine and
Victory over the Turks, detail.
Sala del Senato.*

the island of Crete which
Cicogna had been the rector.
The clock set in this wall is
similar to the one in the Sala
del Collegio, but has a larger
face. The sphere is in gilded
iron; in its centre it bears the
Mocenigo coat of arms, which
may refer to Doge Alvise IV
(1763-78). After this there is
the *Allegory of the Victory
over the League of Cambrai*;
the latter was the coalition of
European states which
inflicted a crushing defeat on
Venice in 1509, only to be
confronted and beaten at
Padua, the city depicted in
the background. The painter
symbolizes the opposing
forces with the bull ridden by
a female figure bearing a
shield with the insignia of the
European states, while on the
opposite side Venice dashes
forward against the enemy
with a sword in her right
hand together with the lion;
the laurel wreath, borne
towards Doge Loredan by
two angels in flight, heralds
the positive outcome for the
Republic. Next to this

is another clock face with the
constellations and the phases
of the moon. Then there is
*Doge Pietro Loredan
Beseeching the Virgin for the
End of the Famine and
Victory over the Turks*; this
work is attributed to Jacopo
Tintoretto, but was largely
executed by assistants.
Lastly there is *Peace*, a
large Tintorettesque
monochrome. On the wall
facing the throne is *Doges
Lorenzo and Gerolamo
Priuli with their Patron
Saints Praying to Christ
between the Virgin and
Saint Mark for the
Prosperity of Venice*, by
Palma Giovane. At the sides
of this are grisailles of
Justice and *Prudence* by
Palma Giovane. On the wall
with the windows is *Saint
Lorenzo Giustinian, the
First Patriarch of Venice,
Giving the Benediction in
the Cathedral of San Pietro
di Castello*, by Marco
Vecellio. Finally, there is a
monochrome of *Ptolemy*
by Palma Giovane.

Antichiesetta and Chiesetta (Antechapel and Chapel)

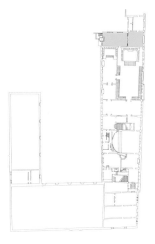

A corridor next to the tribune leads to the Antichiesetta, the ceiling of which is decorated with frescoes representing the *Virtues* executed by Jacopo Guarana in 1766 and partially repainted by Carlo Bevilacqua in 1814. On the entrance wall of the Chiesetta hangs the *Veneration of the Body of Saint Mark on its Arrival in Venice*; painted by Sebastiano Ricci in 1728 this is the cartoon for a mosaic which Leopoldo Dal Pozzo executed for one of the portals of the Basilica of San Marco. Adjacent to this room is the Chiesetta; this was rebuilt by Vincenzo Scamozzi in 1593 for Doge Pasquale Cicogna, who had commissioned him to construct an altar to replace the old one over which there was a painting of the *Scourging of Christ* by

Quentin Massys, now in the Sala dei Capi dei Dieci. Over the new altar in a niche was placed a statue of the *Virgin and Child* by Jacopo Sansovino, which was in store at the Procuratoria de Supra for some time before it was eventually returned to Francesco, the artist's son. After attempting to have it displayed on the end wall of the Sala del Maggior Consiglio, he managed to get it placed in the Chiesetta. This chapel formerly housed the Roman and Greek sculptures bequeathed to the Republic by Cardinal Grimani in 1523.

The walls lined with pews are decorated with fictive architecture by Gerolamo Mengozzi Colonna and his son Agostino; on the ceiling there are frescoes of *Allegories* by Jacopo Guarana.

Jacopo Guarana, Allegories. Chiesetta, ceiling.

Sala del Consiglio dei Dieci
(Hall of the Council of Ten)

Sala del Consiglio dei Dieci.

Returning through the Sala del Senato, the Sala delle Quattro Porte and a vestibule the visitor now comes to the Sala del Consiglio dei Dieci. This magistracy was established following the plot that was hatched in 1310 by Baiamonte Tiepolo with the complicity of other nobles with the aim of overthrowing the institutions of the state. However, because it was discovered in time Doge Pietro Gradenigo was able to arrest the conspirators who were about to march on the Piazza San Marco from various parts of the city, with the evident intention of attacking the palace. Some of the conspirators were executed, others were exiled, while, in order to safeguard state security henceforth, a commission was formed whose main task was to protect the institutions at all

costs. It consisted of the doge, ten senators who were elected annually and six sages, making a total of seventeen members. In view of the enormous importance that it soon came to have in the state, it became a permanent magistracy and enjoyed numerous prerogatives: a secret police force, special funds for paying informers and the power to investigate the public and private lives of those living in Venice who were considered to be a threat to the security of the state, either because of their activities or the company they kept. In his *Diari* Marin Sanudo noted that in 1517 the Council of Ten, which had previously met in the Sala del Collegio now met in the "room called the cage," thus showing that these meetings must have been held in great secrecy.

(above left) *Gian Battista Zelotti, Venice on the Globe and the Lion. Sala del Consiglio dei Dieci, ceiling.*

(above right) *Paolo Veronese, Aged Oriental and Young Woman. Sala del Consiglio dei Dieci, ceiling.*

One end of the hall, the walls of which are lined with a high wainscot, has one end in the form of an amphitheatre. The ceiling was decorated with paintings in 1553-54 by Battista Zelotti, Gian Battista Ponchino and Paolo Veronese.

The decorative scheme of various allegorical motifs referring to the duties of the magistrates in this room may be ascribed to the man of letters Daniele Barbaro. Initially Gian Battista Ponchino was commissioned to paint the ceiling, but the artist himself asked for the assistance of the young Veronese, who here had an opportunity to display his notable talent. The carved and gilded ceiling is comprised of twenty-five panels. In the central one there was formerly a painting by Veronese, *Jupiter Striking the Vices with a Thunderbolt*, which was an evident allusion to the wide jurisdiction of this magistracy. This was taken to France in 1797 and is now in the Louvre; in its place there is a 19th century copy by Jacopo De Andrea. Around it there are four female figures in green monochrome representing *Candia with an Eagle, Morea with Navigational*

Instruments, *Cyprus with a Crown* and *Venice*. The other paintings on the ceiling are now given in clockwise order, beginning with the square panel near the windows: *Venus between Mars and Neptune*, by Zelotti; *Jupiter and Juno*, also by Zelotti; *Juno Offering the Doge's Cap to Venice*, by Veronese (this painting, which Napoleon sent to Brussels in 1797, was returned by Belgium in 1920); *Venice on the Globe and the Lion*, by Zelotti; *Matron Breaking Her Bonds*, by Zelotti; *Aged Oriental and Young Woman*, by Veronese; *Mercury and Minerva*, by Ponchino; *Neptune on his Chariot Drawn by Hippocampi*, by Ponchino. On the wall opposite the windows, above the semicircular wainscot, is the *Adoration of the Magi* by Antonio Vassilacchi, called Aliense. On the right wall is *Pope Alexander III Blessing Doge Sebastiano Ziani after the Battle of Salvore* (the

legendary battle at Punta Salvore in Istria in 1176 between the Venetian and imperial armies, which resulted in the capture of Frederick Barbarossa's son, was always one of the key events in the official history of Venice, and hence was often immortalized in paintings). The canvas was begun by Francesco Bassano the Younger and completed after his death by his brother Leandro. On the left wall is the *Peace of Bologna between Pope Clement VII and the Emperor Charles V* (which took place in 1529), by Marco Vecellio. After the fall of the Republic the hall was used "for the banquets of the civic guard." During the Austrian rule it housed the council of the court of Appeal. After the paintings had been removed, the walls were plastered and the wainscot was painted white. Finally, the hall was assigned to the Royal Imperial Institute of Science, Letters and Arts.

Paolo Veronese, Juno Offering the Doge's Cap to Venice. Sala del Consiglio dei Dieci, ceiling.

Antonio Vassilacchi, called Aliense, Adoration of the Magi. Sala del Consiglio dei Dieci.

Sala della Bussola (Room of the Inner Door)

Sala della Bussola.

The visitor may now proceed to the Sala della Bussola, which was the antechamber for those arriving from the loggia having ascended the Scala dei Censori, that is just the opposite of the present tour.

On the landing of the staircase, set in the wall of the room and communicating with it, there is a *bocca del leone* ("lion's mouth") where crimes against the state could be reported; in the room itself there was a small door which could be unlocked to collect the accusations. The relief of the lion's head was destroyed on the fall of the Republic—only the outline is now visible. In this room those who were to be interrogated by the Heads of the Ten waited under the watchful eye of the Missier Grando, the head of the police. In the centre of the ceiling there is a

copy by Giulio Carlini of Veronese's *Saint Mark in Glory Descending to Crown the Three Theological Virtues*, taken to France in 1797 and now in the Louvre; around it are monochromes by followers of Veronese with scenes of ancient Rome. On the wall opposite the window there is a painting of *Doge Leonardo Donà with Saint Mark in Adoration before the Virgin*, by Marco Vecellio. On the right-hand wall is *Bergamo Surrendering to Carmagnola* and, on the left-hand one, the *Surrender of Brescia*, both by Antonio Vassilacchi, called Aliense. Between the windows there is a fireplace designed by Jacopo Sansovino and executed by his pupils Pietro Grazioli da Salò, who made the left-hand telamon, and Danese Cattaneo, who made the right-hand one.

Sala dei Tre Capi and Sala degli Inquisitori (Rooms of the Three Heads and of the Inquisitors)

Hieronymus Bosch, (below left) *Triptych of the Martyrdom of Saint Wilgefortis, detail;* (below right) *Triptych of the Hermits, detail. Sala dei Tre Capi.*

The inner door (the name of the Sala della Bussola derives from this) gives access to the Sala dei Tre Capi, which is not normally included in this tour, but may be visited on request. The heads were elected every month by the ten members of the Council of Ten and had the task of instituting proceedings. The room where they met has a gilded compartment ceiling with paintings representing themes relating to the magistrates' duties, as well as allegories of the Virtues and the exaltation of good government by the Venetians. As for the two preceding rooms, the decoration was executed in 1553-54. The octagonal panel in the ceiling depicts the *Triumph of Virtue over Vice*, by Gian Battista Zelotti. The rectangular panels in the corners represent the

Punishment of the Forger and the *Triumph of Virtue over Sin* by Veronese; the *Triumph of Justice over Rebellion and Sacrilege Swept into the Abyss* by Gian Battista Ponchino. On the walls are the *Dead Christ Supported by Angels* by Antonello da Saliba and the panels of the triptychs of the *Martyrdom of Saint Wilgefortis* and the *Hermits*, as well as those of *Heaven* and the *Fall of the Damned* by Hieronymus Bosch. Bequeathed to Venice by Cardinal Domenico Grimani in 1523, these paintings were hung in this room according to documents in the 17th century. Previously, together with other works by Flemish painters which have since been lost, they were in the corridor linking the Sala delle Quattro Porte and the Sala del Consiglio dei Dieci. After

(above left) *Hieronymus Bosch, The Fall of the Damned, detail. Sala dei Tre Capi.*

(above right) *Hieronymus Bosch, Heaven. Sala dei Tre Capi.*

the fall of the Republic they were taken to Austria, where they remained until 1919. The large panel painting entitled *Hell*, hanging in this room, was formerly attributed to Herri Met de Bles, called Civetta (Owl), but recent studies have ascribed it to the Master of the Monogram JS. The panel painting of the *Mocking of Christ*, which is evidently by Quentin Massys, in the old inventories was attributed to Albrecht Dürer. This room communicates with the one where the Inquisitori convened. This body was composed of three members, two from the Council of Ten and one of the Doge's counsellors; it was their duty to investigate and pass judgement on crimes against the security of the state. On the ceiling there is a painting of the *Return of the Prodigal Son* in the central panel; the side panels depict *Justice*,

Faith, Fortitude and *Charity*, painted by Tintoretto c. 1566. The painting between the windows representing the *Virgin and Child* is by Boccaccio Boccaccino. The visitor should now return to the landing of the Scala dei Censori where two short flights of stairs lead to the armoury of the Council of Ten.

Opposite
Master of the Monogram JS, Hell, detail. Sala dei Tre Capi.

Armoury

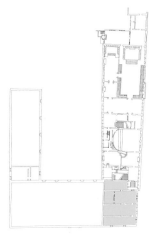

The existence of a store of arms available in case of need was documented in the palace from the 14th century onwards. In 1532 it was enlarged and also occupied part of the old prison of the Torresella. The armoury was closely guarded and few guests had the privilege of visiting it. After the fall of the Republic many of the weapons were lost, as can be noted in the various inventories, but some of great interest were saved and kept in the Arsenal until 1917, when they were returned to the Doge's Palace. The first room is called the **Sala del Gattamelata** because in it is displayed the armour traditionally attributed to the condottiere; this is the first on the right in a glass case, while the last on the left is the armour believed to have belonged to the senator Francesco Duodo; there is also a child's suit of armour found, according to the inventories, on the site of the battle of Marignano (1515). On the left side there are two suits of tournament armour made by the Missaglia; near this there is a brigandine, a coat of mail consisting of metal plates sewn onto cloth that allowed greater mobility. On the ceiling of the following room there is a large Turkish standard and between the two doors of the old Torresella is the armour of Henry IV of France, which he presented to the Republic in 1604. In the **Sala Morosini**, in a niche at the end of the room, is a bronze bust by Filippo Parodi of *Francesco Morosini*, the last great Venetian military leader, who reconquered the Peloponnese in the 17th century and then became doge (1688-94). He was the only person in Venetian history who was given the honour of a monument during his lifetime. In the showcases of this room are displayed numerous swords, halberds, quivers and crossbows which often bear the engraved or painted initials of the Council

Armoury, Sala Morosini.

Opposite
Armoury, armour of Henry IV of France.

Armoury, round shield in gilded leather.

Armoury, morion with a wide comb.

of Ten, CX; the same initials also appear on the doorjambs and are further evidence of the Council's power.

The last room contains a vast assortment of weapons, including a crossbow-cum-pistol with a wheel lock, and firearms of great interest, not only technically, but also from an artistic point of view, thanks to the ivory incrustations and the silver decorations which embellish them. In a separate showcase there is a collection of instruments of torture and illegal weapons (this was because of their limited dimensions which allowed them be easily concealed), which according to the inventories originally belonged to the Carrara of Padua, who were defeated by the Venetians when they conquered that city in 1405. Altogether in the Armoury there are about two thousand offensive and defensive weapons, including morions, burgonets, targets, round shields, swords, broadswords, partisans, halberds, spears, pistols, arquebuses, cuirasses and martels.

Armoury, lamp from a Turkish ship.

Liagò
(Lobby of the Sala del Maggior Consiglio)

Returning through armoury, the visitor now descends the Scala dei Censori to the first floor in order to reach the "Liagò," which is the lobby of the Sala del Maggior Consiglio and was used as a meeting place by the nobles during the intervals in the sessions. When the Biblioteca Marciana was moved to its present home, the pictorial decoration was restored, but not entirely with the original paintings. Above the entrance door is a painting by Antonio Balestra depicting *Doge Giovanni Corner Kneeling before the Virgin*. The painting commemorates the liberation of Corfu from the Turks in 1716 and the consequent thanksgiving of the doge. The city in the background is Corfu and its coat of arms appears on the shield on the right. The saint on the left, wearing the traditional straw hat of the shepherds on the island, is Saint Spiridion, who before becoming a bishop was in fact a shepherd. Near the

painting is a lamp from a Turkish ship surmounted by the crescent. On the left wall are three paintings executed by Domenico Tintoretto in the second decade of the 17th century: *Seafarers Offering a Model of a Galley to Saint Justina*, the *Transfiguration* and *Doge Giovanni Bembo before Venice*. On the right wall is *Doge Marcantonio Memmo before the Virgin with Patron Saints*; behind Memmo are depicted figures of the cities in which he held public office before becoming doge, including Padua wearing a laurel wreath and Palmanova with the star-shaped plan of the city on her shield. The painting is signed by Palma Giovane and dated 1615. At the end of the Liagò, on the left, are statues of *Adam* and *Eve* by Antonio Rizzo; formerly in the niches of the Foscari arch facing the Scala dei Giganti, these have been replaced by bronze copies; here there is also the *Soldier Bearing a Shield* which used to be on the arch.

Liagò

Opposite
(above) *Antonio Balestra, Doge Giovanni Corner Kneeling before the Virgin, detail. Liagò.*

(below) *Jacopo Palma il Giovane, Doge Marcantonio Memmo before the Virgin with Patron Saints, detail. Liagò.*

Sala della Quarantia Civil Vecchia
(Room of the Old Quarantia Civil)

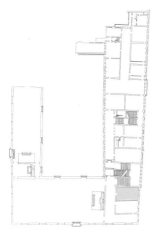

Opposite
Sala della Quarantia Civil Vecchia, (above) *view towards the interior;* (below) *view towards the window.*

Giovan Battista Lorenzetti, Venice among the Virtues Receiving the Sceptre of Power. Sala della Quarantia Civil Vecchia.

On the left wall of the lobby are two doors, the first of which leads into the Sala della Quarantia Civil Vecchia. The Quarantia, the leading appeal court of the Venetian state, was established in the 12th century. Comprised of forty eminent personages, nobles who had held high office, it was duplicated in the 15th century by the formation of a new Quarantia called "Civile," while the older one was called "Criminale"; in 1492 another one was set up: the Quarantia al Civil Novo, so that the Quarantia Civile became the Civil Vecchio. Only members of the Quarantia Criminal could participate in the proceedings of the Senate. Since the magistrates took part in each of these in turn, it was laid down that they should start with the Civil Nova, then proceed to the Civil Vecchia and finish up at the Criminale and the Senate. The office was held for thirty-two months with obligatory pauses totalling eight months. Lawsuits in the city of Venice were dealt with by the Civil Vecchia, those on the mainland by the Civil Nuova. It had jurisdication over civil and criminal appeals, with responsibility for the mint and the monetary system, the formulation of fiscal policies which had to be approved by the Great Council. The paintings were brought here in the 17th century. Opposite the entrance hangs the *Virgin and the Archangel Gabriel*; on the left is *God the Father, Venice Enthroned with the Virtues and Mercury Leading the Old and the Young Enchained* by Pietro Malombra; in the centre of the painting there is a tabernacle with a 15th-century panel of a *Virgin and Child*. On the right wall is *Moses Destroying the Golden Calf* and *Moses Chastising the Jews for their Idolatry* by Andrea Celesti (late 17th century). Over the door is *Venice among the Virtues Receiving the Sceptre of Power* by Gian Battista Lorenzetti (1660).

Sala dell'Armamento or Sala del Guariento (Armoury or Room of Guariento)

The second door on the left in the Liagò leads into the Sala dell'Armamento or Sala del Guariento, which was formerly linked to the Armoury on the floor above by a staircase. Now the remains of the fresco of the *Coronation of the Virgin*, which was severely damaged by the fire of 1577 and detached from the wall of the Sala del Maggior Consiglio in 1903, are kept here. Little remains of the original colours of this Gothic masterpiece by Guariento di Arpo, who decorated the wall of the tribunal in the Sala del Maggior Council around 1365 after the façade on the Molo had been completed. The two large globes displayed here come from the monastery on the island of San Giorgio.

Sala del Guariento, remains of the fresco.

Sala del Maggior Consiglio (Hall of the Great Council)

The Great Council was the fundamental legislative body of the Venetian state. Deriving from the first assembly of sages, was composed of nobles of at least twenty years of age (this limit was later raised to twenty-five), while members of the Doge's family were excluded. The members were appointed for a year, but they could be re-elected providing the obligatory pause at the end of each term of office was observed; this often lasted as long as the period of office itself. The doge and the Signoria (six councillors and three heads of the Quarantia) presided over the sessions. Before the *Serrata* of 1297 the entire public administration was supervised and controlled by the Great Council, at times through the subsidiary bodies, but often directly; later the legislative activity was transferred to the Senate, but the Great Council reserved the right to elect almost all the public officials and to grant pardons. Eventually the Council, in which all the nobles had the right to participate, provided the precepts of the Serrata were respected, became a body formed by members who were practically irremovable. The sessions were held behind closed doors and, at the end of the 16th century, in the afternoon except in the summer; then the order was reversed, probably because there was less business to deal with, so that the most convenient hours were made available for the smaller councils which were overburdened with work. The ordinary sessions were held on Sundays. It was always the bells of the campanile of San Marco which gave the signal for the assembly to start; great importance was given to this detail because any unscheduled ringing of the bells might have caused confusion and led to unnecessary gatherings with untoward consequences. The almost six hundred councillors had to meet in the Great Council under the supervision of the Signoria and the Ten, who had to make sure the doors were closed and that there were no arms in the hall, where only the highest officials had their own seats, while all the others sat on benches placed along the length of the hall, back-to-back in double rows. During the sessions, in the Piazza San Marco and on the Ponte della Paglia were placed armed guards under the control of the Procurators of San Marco, who had to remain in the loggia of the campanile. In this hall the preliminary stages of the election of the doge took place; the proceedings then continued in the adjacent Sala dello Scrutinio. The process involved the alternation of a vote with the drawing of lots in order to avoid the possibility of previous agreements. When all the nobles who were at least thirty years of age had assembled in the hall, a quantity of ballots equal to the number of those present was placed in an urn; on thirty of these was written the word *lector*. The nobles

Jacopo Palma il Giovane, Venice Crowned by Victory Receiving Subject Peoples. Sala del Maggior Consiglio, ceiling.

Sala del Maggior Consiglio.

On the following pages
(p.58) Paolo Veronese, The Triumph of Venice, Sala del Maggior Consiglio, ceiling.

(p.59) Jacopo Tintoretto, Venice as a Queen Offering an Olive Branch to Doge Nicolò Da Ponte, Who Presents the Homage of the Senate and the Gifts of the Subject Cities to Her, Sala del Maggior Consiglio, ceiling.

were called one by one and the *ballottino* (a boy specially chosen for the task) gave everyone a ballot: those who received one with the writing remained, the others were dismissed. With the same procedure of the ballot electors were obtained who nominated 40 (receiving at least seven votes each). Also by drawing lots the 40 were reduced to 12. They elected 25 (with at least eight votes). The 25 were reduced with another ballot to 5 who elected 43 (with at least 7 votes). The last ballot reduced them to 11 people who elected the 41 electors of the doge (each with at least nine votes); the latter needed to get at least 25 votes in order to be elected. The 41 nominated a presidency with two clerks and proceeded to hold a series of equally complicated ballots. From the beginning of the operations the doors of the palace were closed and the electors were completely isolated from the outside world.

Besides Guariento's fresco, the works of the most famous artists of the 15th century adorned this hall which housed the fundamental political body of hereditary patricians, until in December 1577 a fire broke out in the neighbouring Sala dello Scrutinio, spreading to the Sala del Maggior Consiglio. Less than a month later the three sages who had been appointed were hard at work planning the restoration. The first choice to be made regarded the design of the ceiling, which was realized in 1582 by Cristoforo Sorte. Then a start was made on a decorative scheme for the two damaged halls with the

contribution, apart from the superintendents, of the monk Gerolamo Bardi, who in 1587 formulated the programme which was intended to refer to events in Venetian history, with particular reference to relations with the popes and emperors; this would be depicted on the walls, while the ceilings were reserved for the deeds of valorous citizens and battles. The Virtues were to appear on the ceilings of both halls. In the central panels the glorification of the Republic would take pride of place. In 1579 Tintoretto and Veronese were the first to be commissioned to execute paintings for the ceiling of the Sala del Gran Consiglio; they were immediately followed by Palma Giovane and Francesco Bassano. The decorative scheme provided for three large central panels flanked by another twelve, six on each side, while in the spaces between the elaborately carved and gilded wooden frames were to be placed monochromes representing historical events, allegorical motifs and trophies by Antonio Vassilacchi, Andrea Vicentino and Francesco Montemezzano. This imposing work of art was executed under Doge Nicolò Da Ponte, whose coat of arms may be seen on the frame of the large central panel. In the oval panel above the tribune is the *Triumph of Venice* by Veronese. The artist places Venice, who is about to receive the royal crown, on a cloud, flanked by allegorical figures, surrounded by architecture abounding in balusters and twisted columns; underneath patricians watch the scene and at the bottom a crowd

Domenico Tintoretto, Marco Barbarigo. Sala del Maggior Consiglio, frieze.

Domenico Tintoretto, Giovanni Mocenigo. Sala del Maggior Consiglio, frieze.

Opposite
(above) *Paolo Veronese, Antonio Loredan Raising the Siege of Scutari by Mohammed II. Sala del Maggior Consiglio, ceiling.*

(below) *Paolo Veronese, Pietro Mocenigo Leading the Attack against the Turks at Smyrna. Sala del Maggior Consiglio, ceiling.*

Domenico Tintoretto, Doges Pietro II and Ottone Orseolo. Sala del Maggior Consiglio, frieze.

Opposite
Jacopo Tintoretto, Vittore Soranzo Leading the Venetian Army to Victory against Ercole I d'Este, detail. Sala del Maggior Consiglio, ceiling.

mills around between mounted warriors. Certainly surpassing the expectations of the agreed programme, Veronese gave free rein to his taste for dramatic settings and magnificence: thus, despite the contribution of assistants, this work is a splendid example of the artist's painterly skills. The rectangular painting in the centre represents *Venice as a Queen Offering an Olive Branch to Doge Nicolò Da Ponte, Who Presents the Homage of the Senate and the Gifts of the Subject Cities to Her* by Jacopo Tintoretto, executed in 1584 with the help of assistants. The artist depicts the usual elements of the Law, with the presence of the Senators, and Fortitude with the subject cities and the wealth that derives from them.

The other oval panel represents *Venice Crowned by Victory Receiving Subject Peoples* by Palma Giovane. There are many preparatory drawings for this painting; it is notable for the twisting of the figures, which gives them a sense of graceful

movement, and the way light effects are used to bring them into relief.

The twelve side panels will now be described, starting with the ones near the windows overlooking the Molo. The subjects represented regard acts of great valour or military operations which the Venetian commanders brought to a successful conclusion against both the most formidable enemy, the Turks, and Italian princes such as Ercole I d'Este and Filippo Maria Visconti, or else events in the struggle against the League of Cambrai.

The first painting, near the tribune, represents *Antonio Loredan Raising the Siege of Scutari by Mohammed II* (1474) by Veronese.

The following one is the *Venetian Fleet and Army Commanded by Damiano Modo Taking the Defences Erected by Ercole I d'Este at Polesella on the Po* (1482) by Francesco Da Ponte.

The third panel represents *Vittore Soranzo Leading the Venetian Army to Victory*

Andrea Vicentino, The Doge Presenting Otto to the Pope and Receiving the Blessed Ring, detail. Sala del Maggior Consiglio.

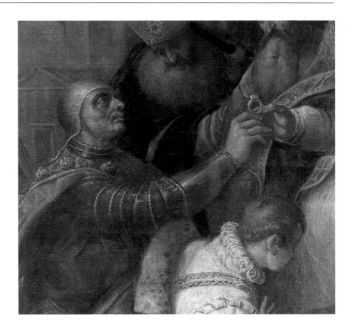

against Ercole I d'Este (1482) by Jacopo Tintoretto and assistants. The fourth one depicts *Jacopo Marcello Dying in Battle during the Conquest of Gallipoli in Apulia Occupied by the Aragonese Army of the King of Naples* (1484), again by Tintoretto and assistants. Next is the *Venetians Defeating the Imperial Army of Maximilian I in Cadore* (1508) by Francesco Da Ponte. The last painting on this side depicts *Andrea Gritti Conquering Padua and Defeating the League of Cambrai* (1508) by Palma Giovane.

Passing to the opposite side of the hall, at the same end, is the *Venetian Fleet with Francesco Bembo Defeating Filippo Maria Visconti near Cremona* (1427) by Palma Giovane. Returning towards the tribune is *Carmagnola Leading the Venetians to Victory against the Milanese Army of Filippo Maria Visconti at Maclodio* (1426)

by Francesco da Ponte. Then there is the *Venetian Army and the Brescians Led by Francesco Barbaro Raising the Siege of Brescia by Filippo Maria Visconti* (1438) by Jacopo Tintoretto and assistants. The fourth panel depicts *Stefano Contarini Leading the Venetian Fleet on Lake Garda against Filippo Maria Visconti* (1440), also by Tintoretto and assistants. Next is the *Venetian Militia under Cotignola Defeating Filippo Maria Visconti's Army at Casalmaggiore* (1446) by Francesco Da Ponte. The last painting is *Pietro Mocenigo Leading the Attack on Smyrna against the Turks* (1471) by Veronese.

Round the walls, except for the one behind the tribune, there is frieze depicting the the first sixty-six doges, beginning with Oberlerio Antenoreo, the ninth doge (elected in 804), who, according to some sources, moved the seat of

government from Malamocco to Rialto and was thus considered to be the first Venetian doge; the last of the series is Francesco Venier (1554-56). The majority of the portraits are imaginary because the original ones were lost in the fire of 1577. Although Jacopo Tintoretto was commissioned to paint them, in fact they are nearly all by his son Domenico. The doges are portrayed in twos, each surrounded by a scroll illustrating their merits and the most notable achievements of their rule. The space which should have been occupied by the portrait of Marin Faliero (1354-55), who was beheaded for conspiring against the state, was covered by a black cloth bearing the inscription HIC EST LOCUS MARINI FALETHRI DECAPITATI PRO CRIMINIBUS. The series of portraits concludes in the Sala dello Scrutinio.

According to the programme laid down by the commission

appointed after the fire the painting of *Paradise* was to be "repainted as it was before." The first competition held in 1578-82 was won by Paolo Veronese and Francesco Bassano, but nothing came of this collaboration because Veronese died in 1588. We do not know how many painters participated in the second competition: certainly Palma Giovane took part since there are three drawings by him for *Paradise*. The winner was Jacopo Tintoretto, who set about the daunting task using a large *modello* which had been further elaborated. The huge canvas (7.61 x 24.45 m)

was painted in the Scuola Vecchia della Misericordia and then transported to the Sala del Maggior Consiglio where it was assembled and completed.

At this stage, because of the strain on the aging painter, his son Domenico stepped in and "finished many things in the *modello*" as Carlo Ridolfi recounts; this is also clear after the recent restoration. The considerable discrepancy between the *modello*, which now belongs to the Thyssen-Bornemisza Collection, and the final painting is perhaps due to the fact Domenico, who painted most of it, gave his own interpretation of a

Domenico Tintoretto, The Conquest of Constantinople, detail. Sala del Maggior Consiglio.

subject that would otherwise have been excessively stamped by the creativity of Jacopo. The canvas was finished in 1592.

The paintings on the walls were executed by the same artists, with considerable help from assistants, in the late 16th and early 17th centuries. They represent two important periods of Venetian history, the first of which is the Participation of Venice in the Conflict between the Papacy and the Empire. Twelve paintings illustrate the difficult phase of the struggle between Pope Alexander III and Frederick Barbarossa. Beginning with the recognition of the pope in disguise in Venice, the story continues with the sending of ambassadors to the emperor, the Battle of Salvore and the capture of Frederick's son, Otto, who intercedes with his father, and finally the meeting between the pope and the emperor in the presence of the doge. Between each scene are illustrated the origins of some of the emblems used by the doges in their frequent processions; here they are ascribed to papal gratitude for services rendered, while it is more likely that they were of Byzantine derivation. (These emblems include the sword, white candle, eight banners with four different colours, cushion, throne, umbrella, ring and trumpets). The series of paintings hangs on the wall on the courtyard side, beginning near the tribune with the *Recognition of Pope Alexander III in Venice by Doge Ziani* by Carletto and Gabriele Caliari (Veronese's sons). Then follow: the *Ambassadors*

Leaving to Negotiate Peace with Frederick Barbarossa, also by Carletto and Gabriele Caliari; the *Pope Presenting the Doge with the White Candle* by Leandro Bassano; the *Ambassadors in the Presence of the Emperor* by Jacopo Tintoretto and assistants; the *Doge Receiving the Blessed Sword from the Pope* by Francesco Bassano; the *Benediction by the Pope of the Doge before his Departure* by Paolo Fiammingo; the *Capture of Otto, Frederick Barbarossa's Son, at the Battle of Salvore* by Domenico Tintoretto; the *Doge Presenting Otto to the Pope and Receiving the Blessed Ring*, by Andrea Vicentino; *Otto Going to His Father to Negotiate Peace*, by Palma Giovane; the *Emperor Kisses the Pope's Foot before the Basilica of San Marco*, by Federico Zuccari; the *Pope with the Emperor and the Doge Arriving at Ancona in Venetian Ships*, by Gerolamo Gambarato; (on the end wall) the *Doge in San Giovanni Laterano in Rome Receiving the Banners, Trumpets, Cushion and Throne*, by Giulio Del Moro. The second cycle, which regards the fourth Crusade, is founded on historical fact and deals with events that were of great importance for the commercial supremacy of Venice in the Orient. The crusade was diverted from its religious ends to serving the mercantile interests of Venice: thus, first of all it obliged the armies which its fleets were transporting to conquer Zara (Zadar) en route and then, once Constantinople had been sacked, it was able, thanks to

the policies of Doge Enrico Dandolo, to obtain "the fourth part and a half" of the empire which was its just reward. An enormous quantity of booty was brought back to Venice, including the four bronze horses of San Marco. The man behind this success, Doge Enrico Dandolo (1192-1205) died, reputedly at the age of ninety, in Constantinople. This series of paintings, which hangs on the wall nearest the Molo, begins with *Doge Enrico Dandolo and the Crusaders Take an Oath in the Basilica before Departing*; this work was started by Carlo Saraceni and finished by Jean Le Clerc. Then follow: the *Army of the Crusaders Besieges Zara* by Andrea Vicentino; the *Citizens of Zara Hand over the Keys of the City after their Surrender* by Domenico Tintoretto; *Emperor Isaac's Son Seeking Assistance from the Crusaders* by Andrea Vicentino, the *Crusaders Besieging Constantinople* by Palma Giovane; the *Conquest of Constantinople* by Domenico Tintoretto; the *Crusaders in Hagia Sophia Electing Baldwin of Flanders as the Eastern Emperor* by Andrea Vicentino. On the end wall is the *Coronation of Baldwin* by Antonio Vassilacchi. In the centre of the same wall is a painting celebrating the victory of Venice over Genoa in the war of Chiogga in 1379, when Andrea Contarini was doge, thanks to the heroism of Carlo Zen and Vettor Pisani: *Doge Contarini Returning to Venice in Triumph after Defeating the Genoese* by Paolo Veronese and assistants.

Sala della Quarantia Civil Nuova
(Room of the New Quarantia Civil)

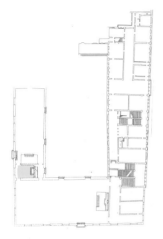

The last door at the end opposite the tribune in the Sala del Maggior Consiglio gives access to the Sala della Quarantia Civil Nuova; this magistracy had the same function as the Quarantia Civil Vecchia, but with regard to the mainland territories. Opposite the window there is a seat for the magistrates; above this is a tabernacle with a Virgin of the early 16th century with, around it, a painting of *Venice among the Virtues*

Entrusting Justice with Lawsuits and Petitions by Antonio Del Foler. On the left wall is *Fame Placing the Ducal Cap on a Model of Venice* and the *Virtues and Justice Driving away the Vices* by Gian Battista Lorenzetti. On the right wall is *Justice Discovering the Truth which Avarice, Envy, Fraud and Falsehood Attempt to Conceal* by Filippo Zaniberti. All these paintings concern the functions of the magistracy.

Sala della Quarantia Civil Nuova.

Sala dello Scrutinio
(Hall of the Scrutiny)

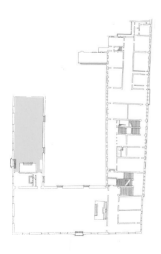

The Sala dello Scrutinio, which is adjacent to the Sala della Quarantia Civil Nuova, was also severely damaged by the fire of 1577. The restoration work planned in 1579 was completed c. 1599. As a replacement for the previous ceiling by Sebastiano Serlio, Cristoforo Sorte designed a composite one decorated with grotesques, herms, and naked figures bearing festoons. In this hall, built in the 15th century, were kept the precious codices which Cardinal Bessarione bequeathed to the Venetian state in 1468. From 1532

onwards the scrutiny of the ballots for the election of public officials was carried out here. The decorative scheme regards Venetian naval victories in the Orient, with the exception of the conquest of Padua in 1405. On the ceiling there are five large canvases: three oval ones alternate with two rectangular ones, while on each side of the latter there is an oval monochrome panel; around the central oval panels there are another twelve mixtilinear panels in groups of four representing allegorical figures, executed by Giulio Licinio. Lastly, on

Andrea Vicentino, The Battle of Lepanto. Sala dello Scrutinio.

the two longest sides of the hall, in lunettes, there are twelve figurations of *Virtues* by Antonio Vassilacchi, Marco Vecellio and Camillo Ballini. In the oval at the far end of the hall is depicted the *Naval Victory of the Venetians over the Pisans off Rhodes* (1098) by Andrea Vicentino; in the rectangular panel near this is the *Capture of Acre from the Genoese* (1256) by Francesco Montemezzano; in the two ovals at the sides are *Doge Domenico Michiel Refusing Sicilian Domination* (1128) by Niccolò Bambini and the *Death of Ordelaffo Falier under the Walls of Zara* (1102) by Antonio Vassilacchi. In the oval panel in the centre is the *Victory of the Venetians over the Genoese*

near Trapani (1265) by Giovanni Bellini; in the following rectangular panel is the *Venetians Commanded by Giovanni Sorenza Taking Caffa on the Black Sea from the Genoese* (1296); in the two oval panels at the sides are *Doge Enrico Dandolo Refusing the Crown of the Orient* (1204) by Giulio Dal Moro and *Pietro Ziani Renouncing the Dogeship to Become a Monk* (1229) by Antonio Vassilacchi. In the oval panel near the tribune is the *Venetians Conquering Padua* (1405) by Francesco Da Ponte. In the frieze is the last part of the series of portraits of doges from Lorenzo Priuli (1556-59) to Ludovico Manin (1789-97). The first seven are by Jacopo Tintoretto and assistants,

while the others are by artists contemporary with the various doges. The wall above the tribune is occupied by a huge *Last Judgement*; this was painted by Palma Giovane in 1594-95 to replace the one by Jacopo Tintoretto destroyed in the fire. In the centre of this a tablet bears Latin inscriptions expounding the tenets of political virtue surmounted by the coat of arms of Doge Francesco Foscari. Above the painting eight lunettes depict the *Four Evangelists and Four Prophets* by Andrea Vicentino. The side walls are adorned with naval battles won by the Venetians. On the wall nearest the Piazzetta, above each of the four large windows, there are two allegorical figures; these are by Sebastiano Ricci (four figures), Antonio Vassilacchi and Marco Vecellio. Starting from this side, with the triumphal arch at the end on the right, there is the *Venetians Defending the Lagoon from the Franks* (809) by Andrea Vicentino; *Pepin Attempting to Reach the Venetians by Transporting his Troops over a Pontoon Bridge* (809) by the same artist; the *Victory of the Venetians Commanded by Doge Domenico Michiel off Jaffa* (1123) by Sante Peranda, the *Capture of Tyre under the Command of Doge Domenico Michiel* (1124) by Antonio Vassilacchi; the *Victory of the Venetians Called in Aid of Emperor Emanuel Comnenus of Constantinople over Roger II of Sicily at Cape Malea* (1148) by Marco Vecellio. On the opposite wall there is the *Victory of the Venetians over the Hungarians during the Conquest of Zara* (1346) by Jacopo Tintoretto; above the window *Vettor Pisani Conquering Cattaro (Kotor)* (1378) by Andrea Vicentino; and the *Battle of Lepanto* (1571) by the same artist. Above the window is the *Conquest and Destruction of the Castle of Margarition in Albania* (1571) by Pietro Bellotto; the *Victory of the Venetians Commanded by Lorenzo Marcello over the Turks in the Dardanelles* (1656) by Pietro Liberi; it is from the gigantic figure about to strike a Turk that the popular title of *"lo schiavo del Liberi"* (lit. "the slave of the free") derives. The wall opposite the tribune is dominated by the *Triumphal Arch* erected by Andrea Tirali in 1694 in honour of Doge Francesco Morosini, called "the Peloponnesiaco" because he conquered the Peloponnese and because he was held in high regard by the Republic following his victories over the Turks. In the panels there are six celebratory paintings: the *Coronation of Defence and Constancy by Peace, Religion Offering the Doge the Sword and Ducal Cap, Merit Offering Morosini the Batons of Command*, the *Doge Accompanying Conquered Morea to the Feet of Venice, Victory on the Sea* and *Victory on Land*, all by Gregorio Lazzarini. The door gives access to the staircase leading to the **Loggia Foscara**.

Opposite
(above) *Antonio Vassilacchi,
Naval Discipline. Sala dello
Scrutinio, ceiling.*

(below) *Antonio Vassilacchi,
Mercy. Sala dello Scrutinio,
ceiling.*

(above right) *Domenico
Tintoretto, Andrea Gritti.
Sala dello Scrutinio, frieze.*
(right) *Girolamo Prepiani,
Lodovico Manin. Sala dello
Scrutinio, frieze.*

Ponte dei Sospiri (Bridge of Sighs)

The visitor should now return through the vestibule next to the Sala del Quarantia Civil Nova to the Sala del Maggior Consiglio; a small door on the left leads to the Ponte dei Sospiri (Bridge of Sighs)—its name derives from the imagination of Romantic writers rather than Venetian tradition—which links the palace to the building of the Prigioni Nuove. It was begun by Giovanni Rusconi, continued by Antonio Da Ponte and completed by Antonio and Tommaso Contino in 1614. The covered bridge, with two parallel corridors, is built of Istrian stone and decorated with a bas-relief of Justice and the coat of arms of Doge Marino Grimani (1595-1605).

Bridge of Sighs.

Prigioni Nuove and Sala dei Censori
(New Prisons and Room of the Censors)

Sala dei Censori.

The Prigioni Nuove, some cells of which may be visited today, also housed the Signori di Notte al Criminal, the magistracy whose task it was to watch over the morality of the Venetians and the city at night. Through the corridor in the Bridge of Sighs facing San Giorgio, the visitor now returns to the Sala dei Censori in the palace. This magistracy, which was established in 1517 and was composed of two members, was set up to defend the integrity of the public institutions and avoid any electoral frauds. The censors were considered to be only slightly less important than the Heads of the Ten and the *avogadori* (the state advocates) and were elected directly by the Great Council. Their sentences could be overruled by appeal to the Council of Ten; they could pronounce verdicts if they were unanimous, otherwise the case had to be referred to the competent council. The

panelled walls of the room are lined with benches; on the frieze is a series of portraits of censors by Domenico Tintoretto and, underneath, the coats of arms of some of those who held this office. In the middle of the wall opposite the window the portraits are interrupted by a panel painting of the *Virgin and Child* by an unknown artist of the 15th century clearly displaying the mark of Byzantine influence.

Palazzo delle Prigioni Nuove, 18th century print.

Sala dell'Avogaria (Room of the Advocates)

Domenico Tintoretto,
Resurrection and Three
Avogadori, detail.
Sala dell'Avogaria.

The next room is the Sala dell'Avogaria. *The avogadori, or state advocates, constituted a long-established magistracy dating from the 12th century.* It comprised three members elected annually by the Great Council; these could be increased to as many as five if required. Originally, they had jurisdiction over disputes between the revenue authorities and private citizens; subsequently their duties were extended to include those of the public prosecutor in trials. Their main task was to uphold and enforce the law, so that at least one *avogadore* had to be present at the various councils and ensure that the laws were observed; thus they could declare null and void any decision which they considered to be in violation of the law. Above the door leading to the Sala dei Censori there is a painting of the *Resurrection and Three Avogadori* by Domenico Tintoretto; on the left towards the windows is the *Virgin in Glory and Three Avogadori* by Leandro Bassano. On the other walls are: the *Virgin in Glory and Six Avogadori, Saint Mark with Three Avogadori and Two Notaries and Saints Anthony, Peter and Jerome with Three Avogadori* by Domenico Tintoretto; the *Holy Spirit with Two Avogadori* by Sebastiano Bombelli; a portrait of *Three Avogadori* by Pietro Uberti. Under the clock on the wall near the way out a Latin inscription reminds us that the administration of justice must be accompanied by circumspection and impartiality. From an adjacent room the visitor now descends to the **Pozzi** (lit. "shafts"). Together with the **Piombi** (the name derives from the lead roof) in the attic of a wing of the building included in another tour, they were the palace prisons where those convicted of the

most serious crimes were confined. Consisting of eighteen cells, they are indirectly illuminated from the corridors, but are not below water level as was commonly believed. The exit from the loggia marks the end of our visit. However, there are other rooms in the palace, adjacent those described, which are not included in the standard tour.

(right) *Domenico Tintoretto, Virgin in Glory and Six Avogadori, detail. Sala dell'Avogaria.*

(below) *Pietro Uberti, Portrait of Three Avogadori. Sala dell'Avogaria.*

Sala della Bolla Ducale, Sala della Milizia da Mar and Sala dello Scrigno
(Rooms of the Ducal Seal, the Fleet and the Coffer)

Pietro Uberti, Portrait of Three Avogadori. Sala della Bolla.

From the loggia there is direct access to the Sala della Bolla Ducale, which derives its name from the fact that it was the office of the *Bollador*, that is the official whose task it was to authorize all documents. Like many of those employed to carry out secretarial duties, he was a non-patrician belonging to the middle class. The Venetian bureaucracy was headed by another commoner: the grand chancellor, whose appointment was for life. The room has been restored with old panelling and portraits of *avogadori* by Sebastiano Bombelli and Pietro Uberti. The adjacent room, called Sala della Milizia da Mar, housed an agency dating from the mid-16th century when Venice began to organize a fleet to counter the Turkish offensives. Comprising four senators and a *zonta* (committee) of sixteen members of the Great Council, it was responsible for the arming of the galleys,

the recruitment of crews and victualling. The furnishings and panelling are 16th-century originals, while the wall torch-holders date from the 18th century. The paintings represent the *Adoration of the Magi and the Queen of Sheba before King Solomon*, by a follower of Tiepolo. A door on the right leads to the Sala dello Scrigno. The most notable feature of this room is a 18th century cupboard; painted with white lacquer and adorned with gilded decorations this occupies three sides of a niche. In it were kept all the records necessary to update the *Gold Book* and *Silver Book*, with lists of the patricians and commoners; this task was carried out by the *avogadori*. On the walls there are portraits of *avogadori* and censors by Niccolò Renieri, Alessandro Longhi and Nicolò Cassana. From this room there is direct access to the Avogaria, or the visitor may return to the loggia.

The Ducal Apartment

Sala degli Scarlatti.

After the fire of 1483, ignoring the advice of those who wanted to transfer it to the opposite side of the Rio della Canonica, the Ducal Apartment was rebuilt in the part of the palace where it had been previously by Antonio Rizzo and then Pietro Lombardo. When Doge Agostino Barbarigo moved in, some of the finishing touches were still lacking. At present this part of the Doge's Palace, which occupies part of the *piano nobile* (main floor), is used for exhibitions and is not otherwise open to the public. However, when designing exhibitions particular attention is paid to the need to leave the decorative schemes of the rooms visible for visitors to admire. The absence of furniture in these rooms is mainly due to the fact that this was the private property of the doge, who brought it to the palace when he took office; after his death it had to be removed by his heirs within three days, and if more time were required a formal request had to be presented to the College. In view of these rules it was obviously impossible for a permanent collection of furniture to be accumulated. Lastly, even if some items had survived, after the fall of the Republic and the subsequent French and Austrian rule, it was very unlikely that they would have been left in the palace. Thus, only the ceilings, the fireplaces and the empty spaces have remained, perhaps resembling the patrician palace from which the newly-elected doge moved (as often as not this was more luxurious) to become *"rex in purpura, senator in curia, in urbe captivus"* ("king in the purple, senator in the Senate, prisoner in the city"). In the apartment is situated a vast hall (Sala dello Scudo) which occupies the whole breadth of the palace from the canal known as the Rio della Canonica to the courtyard; this is perpendicular to another hall (Sala dei Filosofi) which has its only window at the far end and is flanked on both sides by three rooms communicating with each other and this hall. The two large halls form a T; in Venetian dialect this layout is called a *crozola*, that is "crutch-shaped." After climbing the first flight of the Scala d'Oro, the visitor should turn right up another flight of the staircase to reach the corridor linking the Ducal Apartment to the Sala del Maggior Consiglio. The door at the end on the right leads into the Sala degli Scarlatti (Scarlet Room). The name of this room may derive from the colour of robes of the patricians who formed the doge's procession

Sala degli Scarlatti, detail of the mantelpiece.

Sala Grimani, frieze depicting Saint Mark and the coat of arms of the Grimani family.

and who waited for him there. The fireplace, probably by Tullio Lombardo, is an excellent example of the taste of this period for ornamentation based on the art and architecture of the ancient Romans. The decoration, which is elaborate yet delicate, consists of a series of cornucopias alternating with acanthus leaves and volutes between guttae and fusaroles, while the lower fascia contains, in the tondi, heads of putti and, in the centre, the protome of a lion. The gilded barrel-vaulted ceiling is composed of twenty-four panels; these may have been added under Doge Andrea Gritti (1523-38), whose coat of arms appears in the unexceptional painted fascia. The part of the ceiling near the windows, carved and decorated with gold and blue, is by Pietro and Biagio da Faenza and was completed in 1505. Above the door leading to the corridor a Lombardesque relief portrays *Doge Leonardo Loredan Kneeling before the Virgin and Child with Saints Mark and Leonard and Another Saint*. On the opposite wall a painted relief represents the *Virgin and Child and Angels*; on the frame is engraved the date MDXXVIII, which is certainly not when this 15th-century work was executed. The Sala Grimani obtains its name

from the coat of arms of Doge Marino Grimani (1595-1605); this appears in gold on the blue ceiling which is attributed to Pietro and Biagio da Faenza. The cornices and paintings on the frieze representing *Venice* on one side and *Saint Mark* on the other, surrounded by Virtues and Sciences, are by Andrea Vicentino. The fireplace is Lombardesque, with the Barbarigo coat of arms and the portrait of Doge Agostino Barbarigo sculpted on the intrados of the mantelpiece. The stucco fastigium was added when Pasquale Cicogna was doge (1585-95).

The following room is the Sala Erizzo; it is named after Doge Francesco Erizzo (1631-46), whose coat of arms may be seen on the fastigium, flanked by the statues of *Venus and Cupid and Vulcan*, over the Lombardesque fireplace. The frieze depicts putti and arms, referring to his military successes, while the ceiling is decorated with carved and gilded rosettes. In this room a window, next to which a step-ladder was placed, gave access to the hanging garden situated over the chapel of San Nicolò, built by Doge Leonardo Loredan. Through a small vestibule the Sala degli Stucchi or Sala Priuli is reached. The first name (Room of

Sala degli Stucchi, detail.

the Stuccoes) derives from the stucco decorations for which Doge Marino Grimani was responsible, while the second one is that of Doge Antonio Priuli, who added a fireplace surmounted by allegorical figures. Under Doge Pietro Grimani (1741-52) the Senate decided to adorn the room with nine paintings that had previously been in the Procuratoria de Supra, surrounding them with stucco frames. The paintings still present are as follows: *Adoration of the Magi* by Bonifacio de' Pitati; *Holy Family, Road to Calvary* and *Noli Me Tangere* by Giuseppe Salviati; *Agony in the Garden* attributed to the same artist; *Adoration of the Shepherds* by Leandro Bassano; *Dead Christ with Joseph of Arimathea and Nicodemus* by Giovanni Antonio de' Sacchis, called Pordenone; a portrait of *Henry III of France*, possibly by Tintoretto, this painting belonged to Bertucci Contarini, who decided to bequeath his paintings to the state once the male line of his family was extinct.

Since the rooms reserved for the doge and his family were limited in size (the private areas were situated on mezzanines that were completely destroyed by the restoration work carried out in the last century), it was decided in 1618 to assign to the doge a number of rooms above the canons' residence, taking advantage of the restoration planned for the residence itself, which was urgently in need of repair. In order to allow access to these rooms outside the palace a raised gallery 27 metres in length was built; designed by Antonio Smeraldi, called Fracà, this led from the door of the Sala dei Stucchi (now walled up), resting on an arch between the palace wall and that of the sacristy, to the Banqueting Hall, the other living rooms and the new rooms. Altogether there were about ten rooms for the doge and approximately twenty for members of the family and servants on the lower floor. In the last century the raised corridor was demolished and the Banqueting Hall was incorporated in the patriarchate. On the other side of the Sala dei Filosofi there is a room with a vaulted ceiling containing lunettes with the Grimani coat of arms in stone and fittings that indicate that it was not merely used for domestic purposes. Next to this room there is another larger one; the 15th-century decorations suggest that it was from this room, left intact by the fire of 1483, that there was a bridge which allowed the doge to reach his temporary

Sala delle Mappe, Portrait of Marin Sanudo.

Francesco Griselini and Giustino Menescardi, Asia and America. Sala delle Mappe.

lodgings in the Casa Duodo. Probably it is also the room, called the Sala dell'Udienza (Audience Chamber) (together with another two), which is mentioned in a receipt for work on a fireplace which may be identified as the one here: it is Lombardesque in style, bearing the Barbarigo coat of arms and decorated with putti and dolphins. The ceiling is beamed, with gold decorations. At present the only feature of interest in the neighbouring room is the fireplace ornamented with dwarfs and dolphins and the winged lion at the centre of the mantelpiece flanked by angels playing musical instruments. Very often the original appearance of the rooms can be ascertained by reference to the humblest of documents, such as bills, receipts or reminders of overdue payments. In this case, by comparing the dimensions of the room with those mentioned in a bill for the execution of "seventeen paces of frieze" an exact correspondence may be observed between them, so that evidently the frieze and carved panels were made for this room, even though nothing remains of them now.

The Sala delle Nappe (Mappe) or Sala dello Scudo (Map or Escutcheon Room) served as the audience

chamber and, on occasion, as the banqueting hall. There are five windows giving onto the courtyard and four overlooking the canal; formerly on one of the side walls hung a series of paintings by Giuseppe Porta, called Salviati, and Jacopo Tintoretto; on the other there were four maps painted on canvas. The first, called *"dell'Italia,"* was by Gian Battista Ramusio and represented the whole Mediterranean area; the second showed Western Asia and was executed by Zuan Domenego da Modone, or was at least inspired by the one he made; the third represented Asia Minor and Egypt and the fourth, which showed the south at the top, was by the famous cartographer Jacopo Gastaldi, with whom the painter Vitrulio Buonconsiglio had collaborated. Two centuries later these mid-16th century maps were in a sorry state. In 1761 the cartographer Francesco Griselini was commissioned to restore them, an exacting task indeed, involving reconstruction rather than restoration. Without knowing what the originals were like it is obviously impossible for us to judge to what extent the new versions were faithful to them, but the maps were an accurate reflection of the state of geographical knowledge in

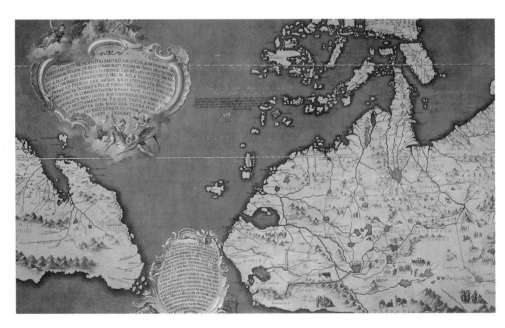

the 16th century and the style of that period. On the wall where the paintings by Salviati and Tintoretto had formerly hung, the Senate decided to place other maps similar to the ones that had just been restored. Thus, Iceland and Greenland, which had been visited by the Zen brothers, as well as the Scandinavian Peninsula, were represented; then there were the lands explored by Alvise Da Mosto: Senegal, the Cape Verde islands and Gambia; also there was the Red Sea, explored by an anonymous Venetian and, lastly, the Americas and the Arctic Ocean near the windows overlooking the canal. The figures and the purely ornamental parts were executed by Giustino Menescardi, who also painted the seven medallions with the profiles of famous Venice travellers, four in the lunettes above the windows facing the courtyard and three in those on the canal side. The escutcheon which is still visible is that of the last doge, Ludovico Manin. Opposite it extends the Sala dei Filosofi (Philosophers' Hall), with a French window at the far end. Under Doge Marco Foscarini (1762-63) the partition wall which divided this hall from the Sala delle Mappe was removed; it was replaced with a wooden arch that no longer exists, while on the walls twelve portraits of philosophers were hung. Originally painted for the Biblioteca Marciana, but not used there, these were surrounded with stucco frames made by Gian Battista Solari and Gian Battista Beretta. In the early 19th century the portraits were replaced by eight allegories relating to the theme of guilt and retribution originally in the Quarantia Criminal, the Holy Family and three portraits of doges belonging to the Michiel family. The Ducal Apartment was directly linked from the Sala dei Filosofi to the chapel on the floor above, and thence to the Senate, by a stone staircase; above the door leading to the staircase Doge Andrea Gritti (1523-38) commissioned Titian to paint a fresco (c. 1523), which is still extant, of *Saint Christopher Carrying the Infant Christ on His Shoulders across a*

River, because according to popular belief those who looked on the figure of the saint would avoid all weariness for the rest of that day. Through the door in the Sala delle Mappe near the canal there is access to the Sala degli Scudieri (Room of the Squires), the antechamber in which the doge's courtiers waited until their services were required. They were appointed for life by the doge himself and eight of them always had to be available. Now the room lacks the original decoration; on the frieze there are paintings by Domenico Tintoretto: *Doge Grimani Thanking the Chamberlain and Brethren of the Shoemakers' Guild and Doge Bembo before the Virgin with the Brethren of the Leather Merchants' Guild*. The large doorway leads onto the landing of the Scala d'Oro; on the other side of this are the rooms of the Magistrato alle Leggi (Magistrate of the Laws). At present these are used for exhibitions and there are no traces of the magistracies which were formerly housed in them; until recent times the walls of the second room were lined with ancient gilded leather, as were, probably, many other rooms in the palace. The third room, the Quarantia Criminal (this is the original magistracy from which the other two described previously derived) is lined with carved wooden panels and has an 18th century inner door in front of the door giving onto the landing of the Scala dei Censori. Two flights of this staircase lead to the loggia and then to the way out through the Porta del Frumento.

Titian, Saint Christopher Carrying the Infant Christ on His Shoulders across a River. Sala dei Filosofi.

Sala dei Filosofi.

The Picture Gallery

In the Doge's Palace there are a number of paintings of varied provenance, some of which are little known. Probably they are those mentioned by F. Zanotto when referring to the Sala dei Filosofi and the way it was used in the last century: "This room now serves as a storeroom for a number of ancient paintings on panel and canvas... which belonged either to this palace or to other offices of the Republic or suppressed churches." The fact that they were displayed in the Ducal Apartment, where a number of years previously the picture gallery had been set up, meant that they were not always visible when exhibitions were held in the same rooms; thus, it was felt more expedient to move them to the administrative offices, where they could be seen on request and would be more protected. From various periods and by a range of artists, these paintings feature religious, commemorative and allegorical subjects. *Dead Christ* by Paris Bordone, in which the figure of Christ appears lying on a tombstone with a weeping angel on each side, came to the Doge's Palace in 1709 as a result of a bequest by Antonio Biondini, a soap manufacturer who collected paintings. In his will he wrote as follows: "To my be-

loved country... I leave a painting by Paris Bordone... may it be presented to their Excellencies the Heads of the Supreme Council of the Ten in order that, if it so pleases them, they may have it hung opposite their tribune." The bequeather's wish was granted and the painting, together with other important works donated to the Republic, was hung in the Sala dei Dieci. The gifts which were not considered worthy of this honour were kept in the Procuratie in San Marco. *Doge Corner Banqueting* by Filippo Zaniberti, originally on the left of those entering the Banqueting Hall, now incorporated in the patriarchate, depicts Doge Giovanni Corner (1625-29) during one of the banquets he was obliged to hold on certain days of the year. Next to him on the right there is the papal *nuncio*, while the French ambassador is on the left. Before the 17th century, when the Banqueting Hall came into use, the doge's banquets took place in the Sala del Maggior Consiglio. In 1423 it was decreed that the doge could not change the established dates: Saint Mark's Day (25 April); Ascension; Saint Vitus's Day (15 June); Saint Jerome's Day (30 September); Saint Stephen's Day (26 December). Apart from the doge,

Giovanni Bellini, Pietà, detail.

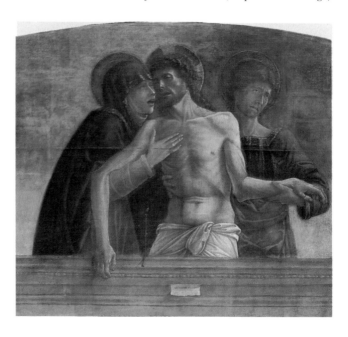

the counsellors, the Heads of the Quarantia (Forty) and the grand chancellor were present at all the banquets, while the other magistrates took it in turns to attend. On these occasions the doge could speak to the ambassadors without being subjected to the surveillance of the six counsellors. The painting representing the *Doge Visiting San Vito* by Matteo Ponzone also hung in the Banqueting Hall. The public appearance of the doge on 15 June, who was accompanied by a long procession of boats to the church of San Vito in the Campo S. Vio, commemorated the discovery of the plot by Baiamonte Tiepolo which took place on that day in 1310.

In the 18th century there were three paintings hanging in the Sala del Consiglio dei Dieci, two of which, the *Circumcision of Christ*

and the *Road to Calvary*, were by Gerolamo Bassano; the other one, *Noah's Ark*, was by a follower of the Bassano. Perhaps this is the same painting as the one attributed to both Jacopo and Francesco Bassano which was bequeathed by Simone Lando to the church of Santa Maria Maggiore, only to be stolen in the 18th century and sent to the Doge's Palace once it had been recovered. In 1926 the paintings were returned by Austria, where they had been taken after the fall of the Republic.

The *Pietà* by Giovanni Bellini comes from the chapel of San Nicolò in the palace. Together with the Virgin and Saint John who support Christ, Saints Mark and Nicholas are present. In 1571 the painting was enlarged with the addition of a Veronesesque landscape by Paolo Farinati. About forty years ago it

Giuseppe Salviati, Resurrection.

Francesco Hayez, Triton.

On the following page (above) *Donato Veneziano, The Lion of Saint Mark.*

(below) *Vittore Carpaccio, The Lion of Saint Mark.*

was restored and reduced to its original dimensions. The lunette depicting the *Virgin and Child and Angels* by Titian has also always been in the palace; according to Carlo Ridolfi and Marco Boschini it was "at the foot of the staircase which from the Cortile dei Senatori leads to the end of the loggia on the first floor": this is the Scala dei Senatori which the visitor climbs at the beginning of the tour of the palace. Since it was practically the same size, Giuseppe Salviati's lunette of the *Resurrection* must have been placed in a similar position, perhaps on the upper landing of the same staircase.

The three paintings representing the lion of Saint Mark come from magistracies which were situated outside the Doge's Palace. The first *Lion of Saint Mark* by Jaco-

bello del Fiore, signed and dated 1415, was in the Palazzo del Magistrato alle Bestemmie at Rialto. The *Lion of Saint Mark* by Donato Veneziano, signed and dated 1459, is flanked by Saints Jerome and Augustine; this painting was also behind the tribune in one of the many Venetian magistracies, which the inscriptions on the book and scrolls indicate as being one concerning the administration of justice. The *Lion of Saint Mark* by Vittore Carpaccio is signed and dated 1516. The date is confirmed by the appearance of the campanile, which was completed, as it is seen in the painting, in 1515. The winged lion places its paws both on the dry land and the water, thus symbolizing the domination of Venice over both the mainland and the sea.

The *Annunciation* by Palma Gio-

vane, executed in the second decade of the 17th century, was hanging in the Sala degli Scudieri a few years ago; later it was moved to the Sala dell'Avogaria. Consisting of two pieces of canvas joined together, this painting seems to have been originally intended for two doors; nothing is known, however, concerning its initial location.

Lastly, in 1818 Francesco Hayez was commissioned to paint frescoes in a number of lunettes for the offices of the Chamber of Commerce that at that time were housed on the ground floor of the palace in the lobbies giving access to the water gates, which had been walled up to form rooms. The lunettes, of differing sizes, were detached and backed with chipboard; they depict Nereids, Tritons, Neptune, another Nereid, Europe, Asia and Africa.

The Doges of Venice

Doge Domenico Contarini (1659-75).

Doge Alvise Pisani (1735-41).

697 Paolo Lucio Anafesto
717 Marcello Tegalliano
726 Orso Ipato
742 Teodato Ipato
755 Galla Gaulo
756 Domenico Monegario
764 Maurizio Galbaio
787 Giovanni Galbaio
804 Obelerio Antenoreo
811 Angelo Partecipazio
827 Giustiniano Partecipazio
829 Giovanni I Partecipazio
836 Pietro Tradonico
864 Orso Partecipazio
881 Giovanni II Partecipazio
887 Pietro Candiano
888 Pietro Tribuno
912 Orso II Partecipazio
932 Pietro II Candiano
939 Pietro Partecipazio
942 Pietro III Candiano
959 Pietro IV Candiano
976 Pietro I Orseolo
978 Vitale Candiano
979 Tribuno Memmo
991 Pietro Orseolo
1008 Ottone Orseolo
1026 Pietro Centranico
1032 Domenico Flabanico
1043 Domenico Contarini
1071 Domenico Selvo
1084 Vitale Falier
1096 Vitale I Michiel
1102 Ordelafo Falier
1118 Domenico Michiel
1130 Pietro Polani
1148 Domenico Morosini
1156 Vitale II Michiel
1172 Sebastiano Ziani
1178 Orio Malipiero
1192 Enrico Dandolo
1205 Pietro Ziani
1229 Jacopo Tiepolo
1249 Marino Morosini
1253 Reniero Zeno
1268 Lorenzo Tiepolo
1275 Jacopo Contarini
1280 Giovanni Dandolo
1289 Pietro Gradenigo
1311 Marino Zorzi
1312 Giovanni Soranzo
1329 Francesco Dandolo
1339 Bartolomeo Gradenigo
1343 Andrea Dandolo
1354 Marino Faliero
1355 Giovanni Gradenigo
1356 Giovanni Dolfin
1361 Lorenzo Celsi
1365 Marco Corner
1368 Andrea Contarini
1382 Michele Morosini

1382 Antonio Venier
1400 Michele Steno
1414 Tommaso Mocenigo
1423 Francesco Foscari
1457 Pasquale Malipiero
1462 Cristoforo Moro
1471 Nicolò Tron
1473 Nicolò Marcello
1474 Pietro Mocenigo
1476 Andrea Vendramin
1478 Giovanni Mocenigo
1485 Marco Barbarigo
1486 Agostino Barbarigo
1501 Leonardo Loredan
1521 Antonio Grimani
1523 Andrea Gritti
1539 Pietro Lando
1545 Francesco Donà
1553 Marcantonio Trevisan
1554 Francesco Venier
1556 Lorenzo Priuli
1559 Girolamo Priuli
1567 Pietro Loredan
1570 Alvise I Mocenigo
1577 Sebastiano Venier
1578 Nicolò da Ponte
1585 Pasquale Cicogna
1595 Marino Grimani
1606 Leonardo Donà
1612 Marcantonio Memmo
1615 Giovanni Bembo
1618 Nicolò Donà
1618 Antonio Priuli
1623 Francesco Contarini
1625 Giovanni Cornaro
1630 Nicolò Contarini
1631 Francesco Erizzo
1646 Francesco Molin
1655 Carlo Contarini
1656 Francesco Corner
1656 Bertucci Valier
1658 Giovanni Pesaro
1659 Domenico Contarini
1675 Nicolò Sagredo
1676 Alvise Contarini
1684 Marcantonio Giustinian
1688 Francesco Morosini
1694 Silvestro Valier
1700 Alvise Mocenigo
1709 Giovanni II Corner
1722 Alvise III Mocenigo
1732 Carlo Ruzzini
1735 Alvise Pisani
1741 Pietro Grimani
1752 Francesco Loredan
1762 Marco Foscarini
1763 Alvise IV Mocenigo
1779 Paolo Renier
1789 Lodovico Manin

Selected Bibliography

M. Boschini, *Le ricche miniere della pittura veneziana*, Venice 1674.

A.M. Zanetti, *Della pittura e delle opere pubbliche dei maestri veneziani*, Venice 1771.

F. Zanotto, *Il Palazzo Ducale di Venezia*, Venice 1853-61.

G.B. Lorenzi, *Documenti per servire alla storia di Palazzo Ducale*, Venice 1868.

M. Sanuto, *I diari (1496-1533)*, Venice 1879-1902.

S. Romanin, *Storia documentata di Venezia*, 10 vols., Venice 1912 (2nd ed.).

E. Musatti, *Storia di Venezia*, 2 vols., Milan 1914.

G. Maranini, *La costituzione di Venezia*, Florence 1931.

M. Luxuro, *La Biblioteca di S. Marco*, Florence 1954.

E. Arslan, *I Bassano*, 2 vols., Milan 1960.

A. De Mosto, *I dogi di Venezia*, Milan 1960.

E. Bassi and E.R. Trincanato, *Palazzo Ducale*, Milan 1960.

F. Flores D'Arcais, *Guariento*, Venice 1965.

R. Ghiotto and T. Pignatti, *L'opera completa di Giovanni Bellini*, Milan 1969.

F. Valcanover, *L'opera completa di Tiziano*, Milan 1969.

Piazza San Marco. L'architettura, la storia, le funzioni, Venice 1970.

E. Arslan, *Venezia gotica*, Venice 1970.

F. Lane, *Venice. A Maritime Republic*, Baltimore and London 1973.

G. Perocco and A. Salvadori, *Civiltà di Venezia*, 3 vols., Venice 1973.

G. Lorenzetti, *Venezia e il suo estuario*, Trieste 1974.

T. Pignatti, *Veronese l'opera completa*, Venice 1976.

S. Bettini, *Nascita di una città*, Milan 1978.

S. Romano, *La Porta della Carta, i restauri*, Venice 1979.

R. Cessi, *Storia della Repubblica di Venezia*, Florence 1981.

R. Lebe, *Quando S. Marco approdò a Venezia*, Rome 1981.

G. Benzoni, ed., *I dogi*, Milan 1982.

U. Franzoi, *Storia e leggenda del Palazzo Ducale di Venezia*, Venice 1982.

U. Franzoi, "Palazzo Ducale di Venezia e gli orologi ritrovati in Collegio e in Senato," in *Bollettino dei CC.MM. Veneziani d'arte e storia*, XXVII, 1982.

J.J. Norwich, A History of Venice, London 1982.

R. Pallucchini and P. Rossi, *Tintoretto. Le opere sacre e profane*, 2 vols., Milan 1982.

U. Franzoi, *Itinerari segreti nel Palazzo Ducale a Venezia*, Treviso 1983.

A. Markham Schulz, *Antonio Rizzo Sculptor and Architect*, Princeton 1983.

S. Mason Rinaldi, *Palma il Giovane. L'opera completa*, Milan 1983.

A. Zorzi, *Venezia Scomparsa*, Milan 1984.

L. Moretti, "Noterelle bordoniane," in *Paris Bordon e il suo tempo*, Atti del convegno internazionale di studio, Treviso 1985.

M. Knezevich, *Il magnifico principe di Venezia. Norme e tradizioni legate al dogado*, Venice 1986.

U. Franzoi and F. Valcanover, *Il Palazzo Ducale di Venezia*, Rome 1987.

W. Wolters, *Storia e politica nei dipinti di Palazzo Ducale*, Venice 1987.

N. Huse and W. Wolters, *Venezia l'arte del rinascimento*, Venice 1989.

U. Franzoi, T. Pignatti and W. Wolters, *Il Palazzo Ducale di Venezia*, Treviso 1990.

Tiziano, exhibition catalogue, Milan 1990.

Palazzo Ducale. restauri dell'armeria, delle sale del Consiglio dei X, della Quarantia Civil Vecchia e Civil Nuova, Treviso 1990.

B. Boucher, *The Sculpture of Jacopo Sansovino*, Yale 1991.

A. Markham Schulz, *Gianbattista and Lorenzo Bregno*, Cambridge 1991.

Le delizie dell'inferno. Dipinti di J. Bosch e altri fiamminghi restaurati, exhibition catalogue, Venice 1992.

K. Brugnolo Meloncelli, *B. Zelotti*, Milan 1992.

Photographic References
Archivio fotografico di Palazzo
Ducale, Venice;
Cameraphoto, Venice

The plans were executed
by Studio Margil.

This guide was printed by
Fantonigrafica - Elemond Editori Associati